WILLIAM WAYNE RED HAT, JR.

"I'll see you again—stahot'sewo'oms."

—*William Wayne Red Hat, Jr.*

WILLIAM WAYNE RED HAT, JR.
Cheyenne Keeper of the Arrows

By William Wayne Red Hat, Jr.
Edited by Sibylle M. Schlesier

UNIVERSITY OF OKLAHOMA PRESS : NORMAN

Library of Congress Cataloging-in-Publication Data

Red Hat, William Wayne, Jr.
  William Wayne Red Hat, Jr. : Cheyenne Keeper of the Arrows
/ by William Wayne Red Hat, Jr. ; edited by Sibylle M. Schlesier.
      p. cm.
  Includes bibliographical references.
  ISBN 978-0-8061-3959-3 (hardcover)
  ISBN 978-0-8061-9015-0 (paper) 1. Red Hat, William Wayne, Jr.
2. Cheyenne Indians—Biography.
3. Cheyenne Indians—Medicine. 4. Cheyenne Indians—Religion.
I. Schlesier, Sibylle M., 1960–   II. Title.
E99.C53.R437 A2 2008
978.004'97353—dc22
[B]   2008009093

Contents

Preface

I first met Bill Red Hat when I was ten years old. We were living in Wichita, Kansas, where my father, Karl Schlesier, was a professor of anthropology at Wichita State University. Having made contact with Edward Red Hat (Bill's grandfather), who was the Arrow Keeper for the Southern Cheyennes at the time, my father initiated an action anthropology project with the tribe in Oklahoma in 1969. His inspiration came from his involvement with the end phase of the Fox Project, which he had had the opportunity to participate in while holding a postdoctoral fellowship at the University of Chicago in 1958–59. Conducted at Meskwaki Settlement in Iowa between 1948 and 1958 by anthropologist Sol Tax and several of his graduate students, the Fox Project is considered the model for action anthropology.

Action anthropology is the application of anthropological knowledge for the benefit of a host population under the principle of nondirective counseling. It involves working directly with the community itself, and thus it can work only if an invitation is extended by the host population. My father's role in his own project was as a facilitator and supporter of the traditional leaders in order to bring the affairs of the tribe into the hands of the Cheyennes. That project helped to facilitate some very specific achievements. As a result of it, the Southern Cheyennes formed the nonprofit Southern Cheyenne Research and Development Association, Inc., which was registered in the office of the secretary of state in Oklahoma on January 30, 1973, and the paperwork for which was signed by eight Cheyenne leaders, including the Arrow Keeper, Edward Red Hat. The establishment of this organization was a response to one of the principal problems facing the Cheyennes (and Arapahos): because of historical circumstances, these two tribes had been lumped together by the government of the United States, and their affairs were jointly administered by the Cheyenne and Arapaho Agency at Concho, Oklahoma. Needless to say, this administrative situation continues to significantly affect both tribes in detrimental ways. By establishing the corporation, the Cheyennes restructured themselves and their traditional leadership to become a representative entity for the tribe in matters that affected the tribe.

My father brought graduate students from Wichita State University, the University of Kansas, and Hamburg University in Germany into his project. He introduced them to the Arrow Keeper, and they worked with him on a variety of topics that were considered of importance to the Cheyennes and to the association. Their collaborative efforts culminated in master's theses and dissertations. During the 1970s, we frequently hosted get-togethers for these students in our home, as well as visits by members of the Red Hat family and other Cheyennes. Once I grew up and left home, I did not see the Red Hats as often. We never lost contact, however, and Bill and his grandson stopped to see me in October 2001 as they were driving back from Ft. Lewis (near Durango, Colorado), where one of his daughters was attending college.

I had been teaching at the Southwestern Indian Polytechnic Institute (SIPI) for several years, and during that visit I talked to Bill about my experiences there. I also shared with him my interest in American Indian literature, and we had a long conversation about oral history and the oral tradition. His visit to my home planted the seed for a project of my own. Before I could ask for his involvement, however, I had to provide the history of what had brought me to this point. My own ideas and thoughts about the project were still in flux, and I think that I was hoping for some direction from Bill. On a visit to his home in Longdale, Oklahoma, in February 2002, I told him that I wanted to bring him and some SIPI students together in a dialogue, and ultimately to bring these Native voices into dialogue with American Indian literature. Bill listened thoughtfully, and we continued to talk, albeit around the periphery of the topic that was at the forefront of my mind at the time.

Over the course of two days, we engaged in conversations that were long and diverse, personal and intellectual, and also both serious and at times humorous. One of our first discussions began with some comments from Bill about the panda Ling Ling, which had been in the news recently. He pointed out that the panda's survival at the zoo was dependent upon a food source that had to be brought in from somewhere else, and that is what makes it difficult to breed pandas outside of their natural environment. From there, Bill began talking about the "white" foods, including flour, sugar, salt, and rice, that are making the Cheyennes sick, primarily with diabetes. This one example from one conversation shows how Bill thinks about and interacts with the larger world, and the impact that this larger world has on his own life and the lives of his people.

Bill also told a story he had heard recently about the Methuselah tree. Researchers have determined these trees to be more than four thousand years old. Only a small number of them still exist. Bill's main point was about obscurity and the role that it can play in protecting these ancient trees from destruction. I could not help but think that he was speaking directly to me in a sense, and how I might be connected to this point about obscurity in my desire to write a dissertation that involved him and the Cheyennes. There is a verbal art to the stories that Bill Red Hat tells, and there is often a purpose or meaning that goes beyond and is deeper than a superficial interpretation. I also know from experience that if I had asked Bill directly what he meant to say in telling the story of the tree, he probably would not have answered my question directly, but might have brought in other elements so as to allow me to come to my own conclusions. This is an important point, because it tells me that for cross-cultural understanding to occur, I must be willing to set aside my own preconceptions about how a conversation should go.

For the next several months, I worked on the prospectus for my dissertation. I had decided to make Bill the focus of the project, envisioning something along the lines of an "as told to" autobiography. Once the prospectus was approved, I sought approval from the university to conduct human subjects research with Bill. I was required to delineate the research project and submit for approval a proposal that explained how and to what end I would be working with the Cheyenne Arrow Keeper.

When I visited Bill a year later (February 2003) with my prospectus and explained to him the goal of the project, he expressed his willingness to collaborate. Even though he was uneasy about the prospect of our conversations being taperecorded, he recognized the need for this type of documentation. During that visit, I presented the approved consent form from the Institutional Review Board to Bill for his signature. His initial response was one of skepticism and hesitation because of the way his official address was noted on the form.

He wanted the sacred center of his tribe to be recognized, so he asked me to include a reference to the Arrow Tipi. As we discussed the change and I edited the form, Bill talked about language—how certain language can be used against someone, and how it can also be used to protect. He said that putting those words into the document would establish a precedent. Bill took an active role in this project from the beginning, and his participation specifically reflects his awareness of the power of words. During this visit in February 2003, we began our taped conversations. Subsequent visits were in April, May, and September 2003 and July 2004. In September 2004, Bill and some members of his family visited us in Albuquerque. Bill's narratives were recorded during the aforementioned visits, with one exception: in July 2004, my parents and I visited the Red Hats during the Sun Dance, and no conversations were recorded during that time.

Acknowledgments

There are many people to thank for helping to make this publication possible. I want to extend a sincere thank you to Hector A. Torres for his advice, assistance, and support. Our many thought-provoking conversations and his belief in the importance of bringing Bill's voice to the page have been invaluable. Vielen Dank, Hector.

I wish to thank Patricia Clark Smith, Elizabeth Archuleta, Steven Brandon, and David Dinwoodie for their thoughtful insights and suggestions. A special thank you to Peter Pabisch for his encouragement.

I am grateful to Louis Owens. My gratitude especially goes out to Gerald Vizenor. I am honored to have his support for this publication. I would like to thank the Office of Graduate Studies and the English Department at the University of New Mexico for travel grants that allowed me to complete the interviews. In Germany, I would like to thank Frank Micha not only for his interest in the project, but also for his assistance in researching some key questions. Thanks to Linda Davis-Stephens for conversations about this project and for sharing her photographs of the Red Hat family with me.

At the University of Oklahoma Press, I am grateful to Alessandra Jacobi Tamulevich for her commitment to the manuscript, and to Julie Shilling for seeing the manuscript through to publication. To Jane Lyle, thank you for your editorial work on the manuscript. Your thoughtful suggestions improved the book.

Many creative writers and scholars have been influential to my work, and I cannot name them all here. In particular, though, I would like to mention the work of Louis Owens and Gerald Vizenor. Greg Sarris's *Keeping Slug Woman Alive* was also particularly relevant; the self-reflexive nature of his work with Mabel McKay has been inspirational to my approach. I have also been greatly encouraged by Julie Cruikshank's project with Yukon elders. Arnold Krupat's work, including his collaborations with Brian Swann, provided foundational knowledge in terms of American Indian autobiography. I have been emboldened in my effort by Elvira Pulitano's seminal work *Toward a Native American Critical Theory*. Crucial to my approach in bringing Bill's voice to the page has been *Telling a Good One* by Theodore Rios and Kathleen Mullen Sands.

My conversations with Benjamin Estrada, Gary Armstrong, and Martin Knanishu about their war experiences expanded my perspective about the Vietnam War.

A sincere thank you to my friends for their insights and their unwavering encouragement. Michelle and Tony showed a genuine interest in my project that helped propel me along. Rusty, Doug, Gabi, Jennifer, Eva, Tom, and Brian provided emotional support during crucial phases of my work. A special thanks to Katja and her philosophy of teaching. I would like to thank my former students at the Southwestern Indian Polytechnic Institute. Thank you also to my colleagues at Albuquerque Academy.

I am indebted to my parents. My mother transferred a love of language and culture to me that helped me to see the horizon of other cultures. Because of my father's project with the

Cheyenne and his personal commitment to the Red Hat family, my work with Bill was possible.

A belief in the importance of family is something that Bill and I share. The impact on Bill's life of his grandfather, Edward Red Hat, will be apparent in reading Bill's narratives. I cherish the memories I have of him. In this context I must mention my grandmother, Maria Kopp Schlesier, a woman who told me stories. She taught me that stories defy our physical existence on this earth. She taught me that despite our mortality, the stories we are told and the stories we remember will go on.

My sister, Sedna, has been an inspirational force. Our trip to Longdale was a personal journey on which we unwittingly retraced steps of our childhood. We literally walked a path and remembered. Walking, watching the dust swirl at our feet, we reminded each other that we had been there before.

To Dorian and Ariane, thanks for being with me through it all. I know it has not always been easy. But as Auntie says to Tayo in *Ceremony*, "It isn't easy. It never has been easy."

Many thanks to Nellie Red Hat for being a most gracious hostess during my visits to Longdale.

In memory of Mary Little Bear Inkanish, who made me a turtle so that I would never lose my way.

I extend my deepest gratitude to Bill for his selfless commitment to the Cheyenne world.

This book is dedicated to our children, Bill and Nellie's and mine and Gerhard's: Marsha, Bryan, Rondeau, Ona, Emily, Eva, Dorothy, Minnie, Dorian, and Ariane.

WILLIAM WAYNE RED HAT, JR.

Introduction

A chickadee landed in a nearby tree, came closer, and then flew away. Bill Red Hat said, "You see, that's good; it means we're saying the truth."

Bill Red Hat is the Cheyenne Arrow Keeper, and we were sitting that day behind his home in Longdale, Oklahoma, talking near the Arrow Tipi in a clearing of blackjack oaks. From time to time, I switched on the tape recorder. I was visiting him in Longdale because we were working together on a project. This collaborative project involves the remembering and the telling of stories. It presents the personal testimony of a Cheyenne spiritual leader whose most urgent concern is the perpetuation of his tribe's cultural identity. Bill never allows me to forget what brought us to this point, or that our individual histories, as well as the larger history, are ever-present. He has told me more than once, "You have to work things out to understand them." Describing the process by which his memories and personal testimony were solicited seems to me the most direct approach in such an endeavor, particularly because such projects often elicit considerable ethical skepticism. Describing the process will also show how our personal histories interact as a cross-cultural experience.

CHEYENNE STORIER

> I really believe in the things we have today. We have had them from generation to generation. We have lived with these things a long time. These things we have in this tipi, we are going to live a long time with these things. We have come a long way with this truth.
>
> Edward Red Hat

My relationship with Bill Red Hat spans several decades. When I was a child, my father, in the course of his action anthropology project with the Southern Cheyennes, would often take my mother, my sister, and me along with him to visit the Red Hat family on the weekends. The Red Hats were living, as they still are, on the original allotment passed down through Bill's grandmother, Minnie. At that time, the Red Hat village (as Bill calls it today) was much smaller than it is today. In 1970 there was an old wooden frame house where Edward and Minnie Red Hat lived. Behind the Arrow Keeper's house was the Arrow Tipi. And there was also the house where Edward and Minnie's son, Wayne, lived with his wife, Emma, and their eleven children: from the oldest to the youngest, Bill, Marilyn, Luther, Eva, Edwards, Mainoma, Albert, Zola, Stevie, and the twins, Pam and Pat.

While the adults talked, my sister and I spent time with the younger children. We played in the blackjacks, walked along the dirt road, rode the pony, and played basketball on the hard-packed dirt. Sometimes we stayed inside to play cards and watch television, or we simply sat around waiting as the food was being prepared. At other times an older Red Hat sibling would drive us into town to buy snacks. Bill was about ten years older than I, and I remember him from that

The Arrow Keeper and his wife, Nellie, at Bear Butte, South Dakota in the spring of 2004. Photograph by Minnie Red Hat.

Sibylle Schlesier, Maria Kopp Schlesier, and Mary Little Bear Inkanish in Anadarko, Oklahoma, 1963. Photograph by Karl Schlesier.

time, although my sister and I spent more time with the younger siblings.

In July 1972, our family joined several Cheyenne families, including the Arrow Keeper, Edward Red Hat, and other members of the Red Hat family, on a trip to Nowahwus, the Cheyenne sacred mountain in the Black Hills. Nowahwus, or Bear Butte, is the center of the Cheyenne world; it was there that the Sacred Arrows were given to the people by their prophet, Sweet Medicine.

A meeting place had been arranged in North Platte, Nebraska, and we all arrived there late at night. The plan was for everyone to sleep in the cars, but some of the children, including my sister and me, decided that we wanted to spend the night in an old covered wagon that stood in the parking lot next to the trading post where all the cars were parked. It was a cold night for the third week of July, and we were all huddled together and wrapped in blankets on the hard planks. The wind whistled and shook the wagon, and the flaps of canvas cracked like whips. It took us a long time to fall asleep.

The next morning, the caravan of cars moved north toward the Black Hills. Our family camped at the base of Nowahwus with the Red Hats and other Southern Cheyenne families; some Northern Cheyennes were camped there as well. We children were instructed to be mindful of our behavior. We were subtly and gently told not to play in the water at the creek that separated the Northern from the Southern Cheyenne camp, and we were not to run, be loud, or listen to music. We were all aware of these proscriptions, but as children sometimes do, we forgot ourselves and had a good time. One night a violent storm took down all of the tents, and we were forced to sleep in the cars. I will always remember Minnie, the Arrow Keeper's wife, standing with her arms outstretched, praying against the wind and rain as the rest of us struggled to gather up what we could and put everything in the cars. The words we heard through the wind were, it was our fault, the kids', that the tents had come down, because we had not listened to what we were told.

I relived moments of that trip to Bear Butte on a recent visit with Bill in Oklahoma. We were taping a conversation when a car pulled up to the house. A young man got out, leaving his mother in the vehicle, and came in to ask Bill to brush the two

of them off because they were going to a powwow.[1] Bill introduced my father and me to the man and spoke at length about
who we were. Suddenly the young man recognized us. He
had been in the camp at Bear Butte; his father was one of the
men who had fasted there. He is a few years younger than I,
but he remembered my sister and me, and how the storm
moved in and blew down the tents. He recalled how Minnie
had prayed, how the adults had instructed us to stop running, that rattlesnakes had come into the camp, and more—
basically the same memories that my sister and I share.

The invitation that was extended to our family to participate in the trip to Bear Butte established a foundation for the
future relationship between my father and Edward Red Hat,
not only personally, but also in terms of the Cheyenne community. The next generation of our families is now adding a
new layer to that foundation as a result of my own project
with Bill.

INSCRIBING PERSONAL NARRATIVES

> It comes to this. Either the object of study is destroyed. Or
> it/they have been strong enough to survive as subjects in
> their own right. They are informants in their own right and
> not only as answerers of questions. They speak first.
>
> Nathaniel Tarn, *Views from the Weaving Mountain*

In one of our conversations, Bill brought up the past, men-
tioning Sand Creek and the Washita. He used his hands—
palms facing inward—to express the amount of knowledge
that a people has in a given generation. His held his hands far
apart at first, then moved them closer together to express

---

1. "Brushing off" is a ceremonial act in which a priest removes from
another person the presence of the sacred. This act usually occurs at the
close of a ceremony or after a period of fasting.

what is lost for the next generation, particularly when a significant group of people in a society perishes. He said that those young people who are still connected to this old generation will retain some of the cultural information and memories, and this is what they will carry forward. His hands moved even closer as he discussed the knowledge of this young generation when they reach maturity. His palms were almost touching when he said, "And this is what I know; this is what I have to work with."

In reflecting on these matters, Bill expressed a sense of urgency about the future and what was being lost for each new generation. He remarked that many of those who were lost "were our teachers, our professors, our leaders." His reflections on Cheyenne cultural knowledge, including his own knowledge, occurred before we began taping some of our conversations, and he repeated those same comments during a later visit after we had started our project.

It is this legacy of the colonized, this loss, as expressed by Bill and shared by indigenous groups the world over, from which the impetus for the salvage work of ethnography stems. The ethnographic and historical data collected by fieldworkers has become valuable to indigenous communities in various ways, and at the same time, the practice of ethnography has become more self-reflexive and critical of its own methods. In "On Ethnographic Allegory," however, James Clifford argues that the allegory of salvage continues: "Every description or interpretation that conceives itself as 'bringing a culture into writing,' moving from oral-discursive experience (the 'native's,' the fieldworker's) to a written version of that experience (the ethnographic text) is enacting the structure of 'salvage'" (113). Clifford suggests that "by opening ourselves to different histories," ethnographers will be able to resist "the relentless placement of others in a present-becoming-past" (119, 115). In spite of what Bill recognizes has been lost, he is intellectually negotiating ways to connect the past with the present and future, and he is also connecting old knowledge with new.

With his reflections on "knowledge," and specifically by situating himself in terms of "knowledge," as an inheritor of Cheyenne traditions, Bill was beginning to focus on what he wanted| to say. His subsequent remarks about the future reveal his understanding of the importance of documentation, which was central to the process we were initiating. When two subjects with shared authority work together to create a new articulation of knowledge, the result is certain to be a compromised cultural interpretation. That outcome should not be regarded as the definitive expression of Bill Red Hat's life or his thoughts. It is also not an authoritative representation of Cheyenne cultural traditions. Bill and I both understand the serious nature of the task and regard it as an impure product, but it will be a contribution nevertheless.

Texts that involve both a Native "informant" and a non-Native collector-editor, identified as American Indian autobiographies, personal narratives, life stories, "as told to" autobiographies, collaborative biographies, or "affiliated storytelling" (a new term in use), have received considerable attention from scholars. Criticism of these texts generally focuses on the colonial relationship that exists between the participants in such endeavors and the degree to which it compromises and distorts the Native voices that are represented. It is certainly true that through the inscription of American Indian lives and cultures, tribal peoples in the United States are subjected to an ongoing colonization because of the assumptions, biases, stereotypes, and historical misrepresentations that permeate many of the texts written about them.

In spite of the ethical dilemmas surrounding such projects, however, they are important, because they chronicle the thoughts, ideas, and lives of individuals who otherwise might not have the opportunity to speak and be heard by an audience outside of their own communities. In addition, they become documents that remind us that the tribes have not disappeared, and that tribal individuals have found ways to navigate the terrain between tradition and modernity on their own terms, and in the process they become the creators of their own identities and futures.

While a collector-editor is not necessarily opportunistic in taking on such a project, traditionally it is the non-Native participant who gains the most from the encounter. In *Natives and Academics: Researching and Writing about American Indians,* Devon Mihesuah appropriately asks, "Why do historians and anthropologists write about Indians anyway?" (8). The benefits, according to Mihesuah, are usually reaped by the academicians and scholars who build their careers speaking for and interpreting the cultures of others.

Anthropology has the potential to unravel the history of oppressive practices. Anthropology can also emphasize global community by reminding us of the diverse cultures that occupy our planet, and that even though we are one species, we do not share a single perception of our circumstances or our fate. Exposure to other cultures broadens our perspective. We need other voices in order to see beyond the constructs we have erected and perpetuated—without other views, we would fail to see the scope of our choices as human beings. I recognize that in some ways this belief is a frailty; however, it is the experience of working with Bill that has led me to take this view of the potential of academic disciplines, in particular of anthropology.

The present project was possible largely because of my lengthy relationship with the Red Hat family. We have a history, and this history is obviously important to Bill, because he often mentions it. When someone comes to talk to the Arrow Keeper during one of my visits, Bill introduces me and summarizes our history so that the visitor knows who I am. This shared history has provided our point of departure.

Bill has given me the opportunity to make his orally transmitted texts the central focus of the project. I believe that he
agreed to participate because he wanted to leave a written
record of certain aspects of his life and his thoughts for future
generations, including his own family, and because he has
something important to communicate on behalf of a
Cheyenne future. I would say, in fact, that his text is a powerful political act in this regard.

My position as the collaborator in the Red Hat–Schlesier
project was scrutinized during one of my visits to Longdale.
In September 2003, in the morning on the day that my sister
and I would return to Albuquerque, a Cheyenne man from
Oklahoma City arrived to see Bill. As he approached, the
three of us were sitting at a picnic table near the Arrow Tipi
behind Bill's house, having a discussion about a symposium
in Kyrgyzstan organized in part by one of the graduate students who had worked with the Red Hat family in the 1970s
(see chap. 18). Bill introduced his visitor as Robert, and the
man then added the epithet "the white man killer." It was
immediately apparent that he wanted an explanation for
why we were there. Shortly after he sat down and began
speaking to Bill, my sister and I excused ourselves for a few
minutes. Soon after we returned, Bill excused himself also,
for perhaps ten minutes. The man began to speak to us about
why he was there, and what the Arrow Tipi and Bill meant
to him. He told us that a lot of people come there because
they need help. He said there are some Cheyennes—he
called them "once-a-year Cheyennes"—who come only for
the ceremonies. As for himself, he said he comes just to visit,
because Bill likes a good visit. "It's a great day when I come
here," he said. He told us that the Arrow Keeper is very humble, and he should be taken care of and respected. The man
said he was there to learn, that he was still a baby, and he was
being humble, too. He was decidedly uncomfortable about
our entire encounter, and he communicated that to us. He

asked us where we lived and what we did for a living. He also gave us advice about appropriate behavior: he said that we should always bring something when we visit the Arrow Keeper (which we always do), and after we told him that we lived in New Mexico, he said that on our next visit we should bring lava rocks, because they are needed for sweat lodges.

When Bill returned, he began to explain who we were. He talked about the students who had come to work with the Red Hats over the years. He said that they had written papers and prepared documents for his grandfather, the Arrow Keeper. He added that the German students wrote the best papers, because they tried to be careful with the language and they carried their dictionaries around with them. Bill told Robert that the relationship between the students and the Red Hats was one of mutual benefit: the students learned from the Red Hats, and the Red Hats benefited from the papers and documents that the students prepared. Because of the students, Bill said, his grandfather was able to attend a national conference dealing with the American Indian Religious Freedom Act. Finally, Bill said, "Well, that's the history." Bill had sensed Robert's hostility, and he acted as a mediator. Bill gave a detailed explanation of our shared history because to him it is important. He has also added complexity to the familiar binaries that come into play in such encounters.

The encounter with Robert was a valuable experience in several ways. It made me realize that even though I had been talking at that point with only one member of the Cheyenne community, the impact of my project would, as it should, extend beyond the Red Hat family into the larger Cheyenne community, however dispersed that community might appear to be. I did not think it was possible, or appropriate at the time, to give Robert a detailed explanation of my motives and intentions for being there. He had made assumptions about my sister and me, and he judged us in that particular context. I realized more fully how important being there really is, and I also understood that I would have to be prepared for some criticism of the eventual end product of Bill's and my collaboration. I think I also realized that the actual practice in which Bill and I were engaged, the process of communicating both on and off the record, was, and in the final instance will remain, the real outcome of our project. The act of being there was more profound than I could ever hope to explain or describe. And I am comfortable with its being this way.

It was always my intention that the project would be given back in a sense to the Red Hats and the Cheyennes as a written record of one Arrow Keeper's thoughts and ideas—not to generalize and speak for the Cheyennes, or the Arrow Keeper, but to give Bill a voice as the spiritual leader of the Cheyennes. Our project certainly would never replace the act of being there; visiting the Arrow Keeper, as Robert did, is perhaps the most important way of participating in the Cheyenne world. I thought then, and still do, that perhaps the project will bring attention to the Arrow Keeper's thoughts and concerns so that Cheyenne individuals might be stimulated to initiate heritage projects in their own ways and on their own terms.

The encounter with Robert also helped me recognize the special relationship that my family has with the Red Hat family. They treat us like family, but that did not make me an insider in this project.

When Bill told Robert about the German students, he emphasized the importance of being careful with language. Clearly Bill is aware of the ways in which "writing" can be problematic. I believe that he also sees writing as a means through which indigenous peoples can pursue self-determination, and I think his narratives will reveal this fact. While the narratives herein are formal in the sense that they have been taken out of the context in which they were orally transmitted, they should also be considered a testimony. Ideally, a Cheyenne scholar or researcher would have initiated this project with the current Cheyenne Arrow Keeper. As Linda Tuhiwai Smith says in *Decolonizing Methodologies: Research and Indigenous Peoples*, "Indigenous peoples want to tell our own stories, write our own versions, in our own ways, for our own purposes. It is not simply about giving an oral account or a genealogical naming of the land and the events which raged over it, but a very powerful need to give testimony to and restore a spirit, to bring back into existence a world fragmented and dying" (28). In the absence of the ideal, in this instance it is my responsibility to do justice to Bill's intentions in spite of the imperfections in the document that will result.

The number of collaborative texts that involve an American Indian narrator and a non-Native collector-editor is vast. David Brumble's *An Annotated Bibliography of American Indian and Eskimo Autobiographies*, published in 1981, contains over five hundred entries, more than one hundred of which are book length, and his 1988 book, *American Indian Autobiography*, adds to the earlier work. I would like to believe that most of the Natives who contributed to these publications were motivated at least in part by the desire to give testimony. Clearly these participants had varying degrees of control over how their voices were presented and contextualized, but I agree with Kathleen Mullen Sands's assessment that we should focus not only on the "cooperation" but also on the "resistance" that can be heard in the voices. It is our responsibility as readers to see, to hear, and to imagine beyond the limitations of the page.

The publication of "as told to" autobiographies, life stories, and life histories marked a turning point in the collaboration between white writers and American Indian individuals: the value of firsthand, eyewitness historical and cultural accounts had been recognized. These texts were motivated to some extent by the idealized notion of recording a Native voice for posterity. For the first time, however, the tribal individual was being identified and recognized as an authority, and perhaps even as a coauthor. These texts were presented as occasions for an American Indian to speak directly to a white audience. In many instances it is unclear to what degree and in what ways the original "telling" was "interpreted" and edited by the white writer, and this has been the source of much recent criticism. Those interested in previously published Cheyenne personal narratives might want to consult the following works: *Life of George Bent: Written from His Letters* by George E. Hyde (1968); *Wooden Leg: A Warrior Who Fought Custer* by Thomas Marquis (1931); *Cheyenne Memories* by John Stands in Timber and Margot Liberty (1967); *The Cheyenne Journey* by Rubie Sooktis (1976); *Dance around the Sun: The Life of Mary Little Bear Inkanish, Cheyenne* by Alice Marriott and Carol Rachlin (1977); and *Red Hat: Cheyenne Blue Sky Maker and Keeper of the Sacred Arrows* by Renate Schukies (1993).

CHEYENNE ISSUES OF SOVEREIGNTY

Manifest Destiny would cause the death of millions of tribal people from massacres, diseases, and the loneliness of reservations. Entire cultures have been terminated in the course of nationalism. These histories are now the simulations of dominance, and the causes of the conditions that have become manifest manners in literature. The postindian simulations are the core of survivance, the new stories of tribal courage. The simulations of manifest manners are the continuance of the surveillance and domination of the tribes in literature. Simulations are the absence of the tribal real; the postindian conversions are in the new stories of survivance over dominance. The natural reason of the tribes anteceded by thousands of generations the invention of the Indian. The

postindian ousts the inventions with humor, new stories, and
the simulations of survivance.

Gerald Vizenor, *Manifest Manners*

As the spiritual leader, the Cheyenne Arrow Keeper defends
what Gerald Vizenor calls "the tribal real." Cheyenne cultural survival and sovereignty are among his most pressing
concerns. While culturally Bill is centered in the Cheyenne
world, he is twice marginalized—once by the dominant
society, and once by the entity through which the Cheyennes
are federally recognized: "the Cheyenne-Arapaho Tribes of
Oklahoma." Simulations of dominance could not be more
explicit than they are in this case.

Tribal politics are currently a threat to the traditions of both
the Cheyennes and the Arapahos. Their cultural survival and
sovereignty are in jeopardy because the federal government
has historically not recognized the individuality of their distinct cultural identities. One result of this divisive relationship
is the various factions that exist within the "Cheyenne-
Arapaho tribes" today. Bill reflects on these matters frequently:

> See, we have two tribes here. We are having to coexist
> with the Arapahos, but we have two different ideals. In
> other words, you're putting, I guess, a Catholic and a
> Protestant in the same building. Now, how do you
> understand that part? [laugh] It's the same thing. It's got
> us in the same hole, and then we're going to try to get
> along to get out. This Catholic and this Protestant,
> they're going to stay in that hole [laugh]. The system is
> separation of church and state, so that's what they're try-
> ing to do here, but in Cheyenne life it's all one—religion
> and living and doing business, it's all one. (Chap. 16)

In a brief narrative recorded on April 11, 2003 (chap. 7),
Bill tells a story that has been passed down in his family

concerning the Sand Creek Massacre (1864). According to his graphic retelling, several Arapaho women aided the soldiers in their raid against the Cheyenne camp. The narrative reveals how present perceptions are shaped by history. His account not only confirms the continued impact of historical events but also provides an insight into the relationship between the Cheyennes and the Arapahos. The animosity conveyed in the narrative could be influenced by historical events, such as the treaties, that forced a particular association that otherwise might not have materialized. On the other hand, the written historical record shows that the Cheyennes and the Arapahos were allied against the U.S. government and its American Indian policy.

Internal conflicts within American Indian tribes are not new. They have their origins in the past, when the tribes were conquered, dispossessed, and confined to reservations. The assimilation policy of the government supported those tribal factions that were considered progressive in terms of the dominant society. This meant that traditional groups who held on to the world interpretation, the religion, and the value system of their historical past were viewed as backward and obsolete, and as an obstacle to their future in changing times. Thus they were pressured from within and without. Essentially, this condition still prevails today. There is no American Indian tribe in which the keepers of ceremonial bundles and the sacred objects of their tribal past are not called into question. The Cheyenne Arrow Keeper is no exception. He and many others across the spectrum persistently struggle to maintain the ancient symbols and to bring them into the future of their peoples in order to preserve their identity within the modern, multiethnic state. The Arrow Keeper offered a quiet response to those who might question his authority and position:

Yes, well, the only answer is, it's sitting out there. They're there. And that's it. So that's my answer. That's the only answer I can give. That's the only truthful answer. I guess if they weren't meant to be here, they wouldn't be here. A lot of people ask me that—"What makes you think that you're who you are?" "Well," I say, "the Arrows are here." So I just have to keep on doing what I'm doing, and that's pray for people and try to help where you can by asking Maheo to help. (Personal communication, February 10, 2007)

Linguistically, the Cheyennes belong to the Algonquian language family, which also includes Blackfeet and Arapahos. The Suhtais, with whom the Cheyennes established relations in the 1730s, are also linguistically related to the Cheyennes, although they are more closely related to the Arapahos (Schlesier, *Plains Indians* 317). George Bent, the son of William Bent (who established Bent's Fort in Colorado in the 1830s), was a mixed-blood who lived among the Cheyennes (his mother's people) for some time. His letters to George Hyde were published as *Life of George Bent: Written from His Letters*. According to George Bent's narrative, the Cheyennes and Suhtais encountered one another on the plains north of the Missouri and made peace when they realized that they were related by language. Their highest priests, the Keeper of the Sacred Arrows (Cheyenne) and the Keeper of the Buffalo Cap (Suhtai), became friends. The two groups became allies, although they retained their own unique customs and their own particular dialects (Hyde 13). The Suhtais eventually became a band among the Cheyennes and intermarried into both the Northern and Southern branches of the tribe.

The division of the Cheyennes into Northern and Southern branches occurred around 1800, when three bands, the Hevhaitaneo, Wotapio, and Heviksnipahis (the band associated with the Sacred Arrows), began to move from the Black Hills area as a result of the horse trade they had initiated with the Comanches, Kiowas, and Kiowa Apaches (Moore 205–50). In this trade relationship, the Southern Cheyenne bands became the middlemen between those tribes and British traders of the Northwest Company. Annual fairs held at Arikara towns on the Missouri River were the primary trading sites. The Northwest Company traded European goods (especially firearms) for horses taken by the Comanches, Kiowas, and Kiowa Apaches in raids into northern Mexico. The Cheyennes benefited from this trade until approximately 1832, when the Arikaras gave up their settlements on the Missouri River. After that date, according to Joseph Jablow in *The Cheyenne in Plains Indian Trade Relations, 1795–1840,* George Bent's trading post on the Arkansas became the most significant trading center for the Cheyennes and other central and southern plains tribes, including the Arapahos. The Cheyennes and Arapahos were the primary traders at the fort, and buffalo robes and horses were the primary commodities (67).

The opening of the Oregon Trail in 1840 also separated the Northern and Southern Cheyenne bands. The split was solidified even further by the flood of gold seekers who came into Colorado after gold was discovered at Pike's Peak. The other three bands (the Masikota, Omissis, and Totoimanha) remained east and north of the Black Hills (Moore 205–50). The division of the Northern and Southern Cheyenne bands would become important in the impending treaty relationship between the Cheyennes and the U.S. government.

In addition to their shared linguistic roots and their alliance in trade relations, the Cheyennes and Arapahos both adopted the religious institution known as the Plains Sun Dance. While the Cheyennes had ancient ceremonies of their own (the Arrow Renewal Ceremony and the Massaum), they joined other tribes in adopting the Sun Dance because "existing religious structures appeared inadequate for the survival of tribal societies on conventional terms" (Schlesier, "Rethinking the Midewiwin" 23). Having examined the ceremony and how it varies from tribe to tribe with regard to origin, purpose, and organization while maintaining certain shared elements, Karl Schlesier concludes that the center group from which the ceremony expanded consisted of the Suhtais, Arapahos, and Cheyennes (ibid.), but that the ceremony must be considered a New Life or World Renewal ceremony rather than a Sun Dance based on an emic view of its development among these tribes. Schlesier deduces that the term "Sun Dance" genuinely applies only to the versions of the ceremony associated with "the Oglalas and their relatives, and the Poncas, Blackfeet, and Sarsis" (24).When the Cheyennes incorporated the Sun Dance as a religious structure, they completed a ritual act that symbolized and made permanent the integration of the Suhtais into the Cheyenne tribe:

> Cheyennes adopted the Suhtai ceremony beginning in the 1750s. Because of the demands of the existing tribal ceremonies, the adoption process may have taken decades. It was concluded when the Cheyennes made the Cheyenne earth drawing in the Oxheheom lodge during the ceremony (making it their own) and allowed the Suhtais to make the Suhtai earth drawing in the Cheyenne Arrow ceremony (marking full membership in the Cheyenne tribe). Both acts are still repeated in these ceremonies today. (Ibid. 16)

Both the Southern and the Northern Cheyennes continue to hold annual Sun Dances. The Northern Arapahos still hold them as well, but the practice has been lost among the Southern Arapahos. Occasionally Southern Arapahos are allowed to participate in the Southern Cheyenne Sun Dance, but more often they go north to participate in the Northern Arapaho Sun Dance. The sacred act extended to the Suhtais in the integration of the Sun Dance among the Cheyennes was not offered to the Arapahos; therefore, they have always remained distinct peoples in the ceremonial sphere.

The Indian Removal Act of 1830 resulted in the forced relocation of all tribal peoples east of the Mississippi. As the tribes increasingly became displaced, their fight for survival took on new dimensions, and intertribal warfare intensified as the tribes were forced to deal with each other either as enemies or as allies. The government used these relationships to its advantage by grouping certain culturally distinct tribes together in treaty negotiations. The consequences of these actions by the federal government affect the cultural sovereignty of many tribes today, including the Cheyennes.

Despite the tribes' resistance to being devastated by the Euro-American forces of Manifest Destiny, the treaties, as "simulations of dominance," continue to have a negative impact on North American Indian tribal cultures. Bill's position in these matters is best summarized in the following excerpt from a conversation recorded on May 2, 2003: "this oral history, this is the Cheyenne way. Tribal law supersedes [Cheyenne and Arapaho] law, federal law, U.S. law. I know there are a bunch of people that would like to fight me on that [laugh], but I think I still would win" (chap. 11). Both the spiritual connection to the land and the spiritual composition of the land are attended to by the Cheyenne Arrow Keeper. In Cheyenne perception, the substance of the land has not changed. For example, the Arrow Keeper continues to make the Cheyenne earth sign in places within the Cheyennes' ancient territory. The earth sign is a demonstration of the Cheyennes' presence in this land, and when the earth sign is left open, it becomes visible to the spirits. In this way the Cheyennes are confirming to the spirit world that the people still maintain the covenant that was established through the Cheyenne prophet, Sweet Medicine, and the Supreme Being, Maheo. The earth sign is taught by the spirits themselves in the Massaum Ceremony. Sweet Medicine made a circular sign in the ground that was taught to him by the Supreme Being and the spirits, and this particular sign is the distinct Cheyenne mark on the land. This act is still repeated today by the Arrow Keeper. Outside of the Arrow Tipi, the Arrow Keeper makes the earth sign to demonstrate that the Cheyennes still feel responsibility for the land in spite of how that land has been distorted by Euro-Americans.

For the Cheyennes, the landscape is alive. Their oral tradition holds the stories and memories of the people as they have traveled. This perception (which is shared by aboriginal tribal cultures the world over) is in sharp contrast to the Euro-American perception of land as a resource to be used and exploited. Claiming territory for themselves was a crucial step in Euro-Americans' development of an American identity and the eventual consolidation of a new nation. In order to possess the continent, however, they first had to empty the landscape. When total genocide was not achieved, diasporas and confinement to reservations ensued. The treaties were means by which the United States could acquire territory in exchange for promises. Those promises formed the basis for the "trust relationship" established by the Supreme Court between American Indian tribes and the United States. At basis, this doctrine of trust responsibility means that the federal government is obligated to honor the promises that it made to the tribes in exchange for taking their land. The scope and definition of this trust relationship continue to be debated in the legal arena.

The history of the official relationship between the Cheyennes and the federal government affects Cheyenne sovereignty, both tribal and cultural. The contemporary situation of the Cheyennes is a direct result of the precedent established as a result of this relationship.

From the beginning, it was never my intention to record Bill narrating his life story in chronological fashion. His narratives were unsolicited, for the most part, and only occasionally did I ask a question that resulted in a recorded response. The methods I employed were an attempt on my part to avoid being overbearing, to be conscious and respectful of his position as Cheyenne Arrow Keeper, and to let him decide what he wanted to say.

I chose a format for our interviews that I felt was appropriate and conducive to our working together. For the most part, Bill decided when and where we would begin to record. When I traveled to Oklahoma, it was to visit with the Red Hat family, and therefore most of our conversations were not recorded. During my winter visits, the taped conversations took place in his home; in the fall and spring, we often sat outside near the Arrow Tipi. Sometimes Bill would motion for me to turn the tape recorder on, and sometimes I would initiate the process. I rarely interrupted him, and only occasionally did I ask questions. In this way, I was able to collect what often became rather lengthy, sustained narratives. On some occasions a taping session was interrupted for various reasons, because someone came to visit the Arrow Keeper, or family members came for a visit, or the conversation turned to something that he did not want recorded. Some of the narratives are thus rather brief. I have retained the order of the narratives as they were recorded in the course of five visits. The transcriptions have been only minimally edited; I occasionally changed grammatical constructions or repetitions, but in most cases I retained these characteristics of his speech. Some minor changes were made in the narratives after the initial taping in accordance with Bill's wishes. This is also one reason why in some instances names have been changed to initials in order to protect an individual's identity.

Tape-recorded conversations are, of course, unnatural to a degree. There was a detectibly different purpose to Bill's speaking when the tape was running. It can certainly be argued that there is a contrived quality to any narrative that

Bill Red Hat and Sibylle Schlesier during a visit in Corrales, New Mexico, in the fall of 2004. Photograph by Karl Schlesier.

is recorded. This fact seems unavoidable to some extent and did not deter either of us in our desire to continue in the manner in which we set out. We were also following a tradition, in the sense that several graduate students had tape-recorded his grandfather in the 1970s, and those tapes remain important to Bill. He listens to them often, and during one of my visits he played one of the tapes, stopping at intervals both to translate the Cheyenne and to comment on what his grandfather was saying. I therefore think he considers the mode we employed to be a useful form of documentation.

Bill prepared himself formally before we began the first of our taped sessions. He left the house, and when he returned, he had painted himself—this was the outward expression through which he conveyed to me his recognition of the formality of our collaboration and the solemnity with which he would approach the project. As readers will gather from his narratives, Bill speaks a great deal about truth. Truth is intrinsic to his position as Arrow Keeper, and it is a guiding principle in his life. He must tell the truth because the Arrows are with him. It is not my responsibility to define truth. It is the reader's responsibility to listen and to hear what Bill says. As Vizenor says, "What has been published and seen is not what is heard or remembered in oral stories," and "The sudden closures of the oral in favor of the scriptural are unheard, and the eternal sorrow of lost sounds haunts the remains of tribal stories in translation" (*Manifest Manners* 70, 69). I do not want to misrepresent a tribal, Cheyenne consciousness, and thus I must be silent on some matters. Bill's contribution to our collaboration is rooted in the aural, and I must attempt to privilege this fact.

CHAPTER 1

"I Went through It"

February 7, 2003

Well, anyway, I thought about it, and what would my grandpa say? Because he would want to be right there, and he's always been right there, to pick me up, to give me a pep talk, whatever I needed. And I kept wondering, how was he able to do the things he did here? I know he would want to go to Vietnam, and if somebody shot at me he would try to get in the way, but the bullets would just tear him up, too.[1] So I just kept thinking about that—that he would want to be there. But then this is the reality, this is experience, this is life, this is what goes on, and you can't be there all the time. You would want to be. So how would my grandpa stop these bullets, or how would he pray for the bullets to go by, or what would he do to protect me? The only thing that I've come up with is that all he had to do was pray. And he didn't pray that

---

1. A great deal has been written about Native war veterans. Two recent books that contextualize the American Indian Vietnam experience are *Strong Hearts, Wounded Souls: Native American Veterans of the Vietnam War* by Tom Holm, and Woody Kipp's personal narrative, *Viet Cong at Wounded Knee: The Trail of a Blackfeet Activist.*

the bullets would miss me; he prayed that if they hit me, that I would somehow come through. So this is what every parent's prayers should be, is that you can't stop it but you can pray that whatever your children run into, whatever problems arise in front of them, the only thing you can pray is that they will successfully come through it. It's the only way you can pray. This is what I thought, because my grandpa couldn't be there with me.

When I went to Vietnam, I wondered how he could help me. He prayed that I would come through this, because you can't stop these things.

When I came back, it was bad dreams, it was just bad things, but it was just something I couldn't chase away. I couldn't fight it, I couldn't beat it up, I couldn't get it out of my system. It was always there, and the only thing to get it away was to drink until you passed out. You know, when you pass out, you don't have any kind of dreams. That was just what you had to do, so I think for about two years, that's all I did was drink. You had to be busy so that you couldn't think about that.

It brought it back, not too long ago, about a month and a half ago. My Uncle Henry died. He drank himself to death. Well, I don't know; he had other problems, too. Anyway, I went to his funeral, and I went up to talk. The thing that came to me was that he was still drinking, in 2002. I quit in '74 or '75. Most people look at them as drunks. It really brought it back, because he had seen the things that I had seen. It's when your friends, their blood and guts are just splattered, and then it's warm when that thing hits you; it's almost hot, not real hot, but hot, and then all at once it cools down, and then it cakes. When you're in the field, you can't wash; you're like in the desert, and you just get a stick and try to brush that stuff off. And then you have to eat, and the sun gets real hot by about nine o'clock in the morning, and you have to eat, and it's all over your legs. But you have to eat, and you have to get things ready, or ready to move out, and then you eat, and you taste that and you can't get rid of it, and you smell that. And even when you have a bloody nose, it all comes back to you. And you want to try to get away from it, but the only way is to drink. You can't smoke or you can't do drugs because you might get high, but you still have your functioning senses with you, and you can still feel it.

It's things that you learn [how and why to do drugs]. You're subject to things. These other guys, they found that out, and so they're trying to help you and they give you something—"Here, take this, you'll be all right." Because you're worried about the bullet coming, or about getting hit. And you don't really care if you get hit if you just got there, but if you're ready to come home, man, you're shaking, you're scared. You just do what the situation allows. It's not something you want to do. You're put into that situation, and they'll turn around and arrest you for it and throw you into the brig, and your life is messed up, and they're not trying to help you. They're your officers, they're your chain of command, they're your people, they're supposed to be trying to help you. The officials are not looking at it; they're not trying to help you. They allow it, but if you drink too much, then they come down on you, the whole system comes down on you, and they can throw people out and ruin them for the rest of their lives, when all they needed to do was understand . . . Just like my grandpa, he couldn't be there, but the only thing he had was a prayer back here, and that's all they needed to do. They just needed to contact everyone in the United States and tell them to pray a certain way, every day for so many days, and that you can't stop it but you can pray that they come through it. And so that's what I thought about what my grandpa had to do, because he couldn't stop these bullets.

My first time I was in Dong Ha, Third Marine Division, Third Battalion, and then I went to a fire base called Ca Lu, and I was there for a couple of months. I was with a weapons

platoon, 60 millimeter mortars. So I was with a weapons platoon, but we would always go out with the captain. When we
got to Phu Bai, we got there on the C-130. They lowered the
back end of the plane, and hot air just came in. You could
hardly breathe, it was so hot. The tar on the runway and the
diesel smell—boy, it was hot. They outfitted us at Dong Ha.
They gave us our helmets and equipment, and we took a con-
voy ride from Dong Ha to Ca Lu. When we got there, I asked
my squad leader when I would get a rifle. He said, "Where's
your rifle? They sent you out here without a rifle? What were
you going to do if you guys got hit?" So we finally got outfitted, and then you got put with your platoon. There were three
squads there. Then you moved into the bunkers and got a cot
and put your stuff in there. There were rats in there. That was
your place. That's where you would be operating from.

In Ca Lu, I actually killed my first enemy there. I had been
in the country about two or three months. They have what
they call H and I's—harassment and interdictory fire—in a
perimeter. You're in a certain place at night, and you go on
watch two hours each. So you pick a place where you're
going to shoot. You don't tell anyone; you just write it down
for yourself. Once you write it down, they tell you the night
before where the ambushes are going to be, and you can't
fire where these groups are. You fire the mortar at night.
There's no pattern; it's random. Sometimes troops come by,
and you could accidentally hit them. So I fired that night my
second round, about six hundred yards out. It came close to
an ambush team, and they heard a scream. So they just
stayed there. The next morning there was commotion all at
once, and people and officials were running around, and the
squad comes walking in carrying a body. The section leaders
are all saying, "What did you shoot last night? Where did
you shoot? Where did you hit?" So they went around and
asked everyone, and they made it look like we hit the
ambush. They asked us whether we knew that the ambush

was out there. Then they would, just to scare you, they would just play along like you had done something wrong. At the same time, these other guys are running back and forth bringing this body in, carrying this body, and they have a poncho over him and you can't see who it is. But the ambush is coming in, and you don't know how many went out on the ambush, whether it was six or seven; and you're scared because somebody did something—somebody either hit the ambush team or something.

So they brought him in, and pretty soon the platoon commander left and came back and went into his hooch and yelled, "Red Hat, front and center!" And everybody looked at you and said, "Oh, man, Red Hat, you're going down!" Because we thought we hit one of our ambush guys. So I walked over there and knocked on his door, and he told me to come in. He asked, "Where did you fire last night?" He was sitting over his little ammo-box desk as I was coming in the door. So I had a piece of paper to show him where I fired, and he looked at it and put his head down for a while, and then he looked up at me and he started smiling and said, "Congratulations! You got your first one last night." "What?" I said. "You killed your first enemy last night. He was by himself." My round hit him right between his legs. The commander shook my hand. Everyone else out there knew already, and they all patted me on the back and everything, and then I was sick inside. You were trying to be macho and everything like everyone else, but there was something here [touching his chest] that was bothering me. I was talking like they were talking, but after a while you get over it.

About a month and a half later, on November tenth, on the Marine Corps' birthday, is when I was wounded. Well, actually it was at 12:30, just past midnight on the eleventh. So I always tell people I got wounded one time on two days. I had about forty shrapnel wounds. I got hit by a mortar also, like the one I hit the guy with. So what goes around comes around.

We had a fire mission, and my gun was directly behind the skipper. He called a fire mission, and then we fired 360 degrees straight north. And we hit one gun, and the guys hollered back to us, "You hit it!" But this guy was a decoy, and this other one opened up at 78 degrees, close to the one we hit. The skipper hollered back to us, "Seventy-eight degrees!" So I turned my gun around to 78 degrees, and I held three rounds of mortar, and I dropped the first one in, getting ready to put the second one in, and then all I saw was a flash. I saw a real bright light, and I can't remember if I got the second one in. By the time I raised my hand up, one of the rounds hit me on the hand, close to the mortar I was holding in that hand. If it had hit the mortar, it would have exploded. It hit about five feet behind me. I saw a picture of my family when the flash went off. It didn't seem like long. I saw my grandpa, and my life, and it was all in a flash, just coming. It happened so quick. Here's what I felt like: There was a boy that shot a cat one time. We were kids. It was a preacher's son, and he shot a cat in the back. And as soon as the cat got shot, the cat went back and started scratching at the fur, swinging at his back, and then he took off. In that same instant, that's what I think I did. I don't know if I did that, but that's what I think I did. Because that's the picture that came. In my mind I could see the blast, the hot metal flying in all directions. Then my whole body was numb, and I could see all of my life, and my grandma and grandpa, my parents, and all the kids, everyone. I could see them.

The next thing I know, I was laying on my side, and the guy who was on the side of me was hit in the face and in the leg. I was lying there, and I had dug a small hole. And I tried to get up, but my hand was broken and my left leg was fractured. And we started hearing the guns again; they were coming again. I don't know how I did it, but I dragged myself into the hole, and I hurt my shoulder, but I fell into the hole, and pulled my legs into the hole, and the next thing I knew, some guys were picking me up. They were hurting my arm but they were running with me, and we ran to an old church, about forty to fifty yards away. So they laid us down in there, and that was the longest night of my life. They cut our clothes and started putting bandages on our arms and legs, and they said they couldn't give me any water. Because what they thought was when this thing came up, that it shredded my jacket. When it shredded my flak jacket, they thought that some of it went into my belly because there was blood all over. I laid there until about 7:30 in the morning. I had my legs crossed. The blood was pooling on the side of my body.

That afternoon, on the tenth, it was raining, and they brought in hot chow for the Marine Corps' birthday. We got milk, beer, hot food, so we ate that. Then an army plane came flying around us. It was a spotter plane and had red smoke. He put down his window: "Happy Birthday, Marines! Happy Birthday, Marines!" That was the worst thing he could have done. Because by the time the birthday was over, they were waiting on us. That day it was about three or four o'clock. There was one guy. He was in a rice paddy, or a crop. I heard an explosion. I saw like a rag floating in the air. All the time it was this guy. He hit the ground and some of the guys said, "Watch out, booby trap!" He had stepped on an anti-tank mine. What they would do is file the fire pins loose so that a man's weight could set it off. But it didn't kill him. He was all black and his clothes were all shredded, and he had blood coming out of his ears.

So anyway, the next morning they carried me and another guy from our unit to the helicopter. There were bodies lined up with ponchos over them, and some other wounded guys. So I was the first one they put on the helicopter. They put us on our stretchers and tied us down, and the helicopter took off. You could hear the bullets pinging against the helicopter, but it got up. It got a little elevation and took off. Then we got to Dong Ha, and they still wouldn't give us any water. Well, the chaplain came in and I said, "Father, I need some water." They had told him not to give us anything, and so he took a piece of gauze soaked in water and he gave me that. I felt pretty good, and he already started writing a letter to my parents. He signed it for me. He asked me what the address was.

They operated on me. They cut away all of the burned black flesh. The surgeon told me that I would have bled to death. They gave me three pints of blood. The surgeon said that if the mortar had been further away, it would have killed me, but since it was about five feet behind me, it was still white-hot, and so when it went into the skin it cauterized. And that's what saved me, that it was so close. It fused itself shut. I still bled a lot. Anyway, it was the longest night of my life. I saw my whole family. I didn't think I could die. I don't think I thought about dying. I was more in pain. I was hurt. I had too many guys around me. They sent me to Da Nang, where they did some other stuff, and then to Phu Bai, the Philippines. The funny thing about that, being in these different places, your records get lost, and they give you shots for the pain. By the time my records caught up with me, I had already been on Demerol for two weeks. I got hooked on Demerol. When I was lying in the hospital, after about three or four hours I started paining. I couldn't hardly take it. These black guys across the room from me would say, "Hey, he's going under again," so they would put on some music. So we kind of got a talking rapport and knowing each other, and they'd say, "Play some jazz for him."

I stayed for thirty days, and then everything healed up, and then they sent me back to the same place. From Yokosuka they sent me back.

I went to headquarters, Ninth Marines. It was security for convoys to take food out there. So that's all we did until Khe Sanh got shut down, and then they put me into another outfit, Third Battalion, Fourth Marines. Then I finished out my tour there.

The last three or four days of my thirteen months there, then I got scared. That day I heard them call. The skipper said, "Hey, they want Whiskey Whiskey Romeo Hotel [William Wayne Red Hat]." I heard them say I had a flight date. Everybody said, "Hey, Red Hat, they're talking about you." So I started digging a hole that evening. I put my flak jacket over the top of it, and I sat there with my rifle and said, "Don't bother me. Don't come call me to do anything." So that evening they came. They brought supplies in that evening. There was a dog handler and a dog on the helicopter, and he wasn't going to get off. But I got on there and I threw the dog off, and he had to jump off. So I got on.

I was happy when I left. When we got into the airplane, the stewardesses brought hot towels and gave them to all of us, and we started washing ourselves off. They were all black and red, and some of the guys were afraid to give them back to the stewardesses. The pilot took off and he said, "I'm going to bank left. Everybody look down; this is the last time you're going to see it." He banked and let us look at it.

So I came home. I took a cab from Oklahoma City, forty-five dollars to bring me home from there.

I still served out. I went back for another tour. When I left there, there was something that was going on with my mind. I couldn't take orders from another man unless he had killed an enemy.[2] I couldn't take orders from anyone who hadn't done what I had done. So when I got back here, I got into trouble. I went UA [unauthorized absence] for 30 days. Another guy, a white kid that I knew, missed 85 days.

2. In the Cheyenne past, the only persons of authority who were able to give orders (limited, however, to situations in military conflict) were the headmen of warrior societies. Their orders were followed because of the headmen's personal experience in warfare, their insights and tactical skills. Cheyenne headmen were expected to die young, and many did in fact die young. Those who survived usually became renowned band or tribal chiefs or ceremonial leaders in later life.

Another kid left 116 days. These guys got office hours. They busted me down, took all my rank, and threw me in the brig for three months. I signed to go back after I got out of the brig. Then I went back as a private. They sent me out into the First Marine Division because they were pulling the Third Marine Division out.

Here's what's funny about this. Nixon said he was going to bring home the Third Marine Division. So he did bring the Third Marine Division out. But what he did was, these guys that were ready to rotate on the First Marine Division, he put them there; and the new ones that were here, he turned around and put them back here. So he didn't do anything for anybody but bring back the ones that were ready to come home anyway. So they put me back there because I had thirteen months to go.

Anyway, when I got there, like I said, I couldn't take orders. It's a real thing that needs to be dealt with.

We went to different places. Barrier Island. Hill 55. Antenna Valley. That's where a lot of people didn't make it out. It's between two mountains. I did my thirteen months. Then I came home.

It takes time. I'm glad my grandpa was there. He got me out of all that. It took time. Like my Uncle Henry. He was with the Airborne. I didn't realize anything that much about it, but it was still bothering him. But most people thought he was just a drunk. It's like what they do to people; they just forget about them, they just throw them away.

I learned there is prejudice. I went through it. A lot of that prejudice by being busted down so many times is because of prejudice, because of some lieutenant or some sergeant.

These experiences have led me to what I'm doing. It has prejudice, it has the authority, where authority does things wrong. But I think I had to have that to get where I'm at today. I think that's what built me so far. Now I know who is on whose side.

CHAPTER 2

"You Have to Know These Things"

February 7, 2003

On June 22, 1990, from about two o'clock in the afternoon to seven o'clock that evening, we went to the ceremonial grounds.[1] There was a lot of trouble going on. A whirlwind had come by, and L. H.'s three tipis were sitting up on the northeast side, and the whirlwind had knocked his tipis down and then came by our tipi and knocked L. W.'s tipi down. And so we went on up there and we asked them what happened, and they told us that story. My dad had sent word to the Lone Tipi, where A. H., W. F., and several Sun Dance priests and members of societies were inside.[2] We were in my dad's shade, and my dad sent word over there to call him in, and he never came. So I was kind of worried, and time was

1. The Cheyenne ceremonial grounds where the camps assemble in summer for the Oxheheom, a World Renewal Ceremony often called the Sun Dance, and the Maxhoetonstov, the Arrow Ceremony, are an old Cheyenne allotment at the edge of the town of Seiling, Oklahoma.
2. The first day of the Oxheheom takes place in the "Lone Tipi." The ancient giving of the ceremony to Erect Horns and the Sacred Woman is reenacted in the Lone Tipi, and the main performers are instructed regarding their roles and obligations during the three days of the public display.

going by, so I called my son Bryan to go over there. So I did what I was supposed to do to protect him—I put a sheet on him. "See your uncle out there? Go out there and tell your uncle that A. H. needs to come over here; a headsman is calling." My dad is an Omaha Society Clan headsman, and a headsman has a right to do some of these things if they are telling the truth.[3] But if they are not telling the truth, then they don't have a right to do certain things.

So my dad was telling the truth, and A. H. didn't come out. So I took the protection off of my son, and he went and played. About twenty or thirty minutes later, I called Bryan back, and I had to put protection on him again so that he could go over to the Tipi and tell A. H. to come talk to the headsman. I was an Arrow Priest at that time, and there were other headsmen there, and society members: Edwards Red Hat and J. B. So Bryan went back up there to do that, and I took everything off him again, and he went and played. And so we waited. Our long-time friend K. H. S. and C. F. were there also, and we were just standing around talking in the shade, and there were different people, relatives, talking in the shade. And then A. H. finally came out, and he was coming towards the shade. I told my dad, "You have to stop him out there; you can't let him come in the shade." That's the procedure.

My dad went out from the shade, and he and A. H. sat down on the ground. In the meantime, four society members came and sat down behind A. H. to listen. One was S. H., and also B. B., S. B., and V. B. were there. Then my dad told A. H., "You stopped my son from fulfilling his ceremony. You've been a crier in funerals. You've put sage in the coffins when they bury the people. You've been drinking with the

---

3. Because of their function to protect the people against whatever danger, warrior society headmen have the authority to question judgments made by the chiefs and ceremonial persons.

Arrows.[4] You've been bossing the societies around telling them what to do, and you've been going to the drum, singing at the drum. And you've given the Arrows to S. A., a Northern Cheyenne. All of these things aren't allowed. Now you are being asked by a headsman whether you have done all of these things." He was looking for a stick—he needed a stick to point with and to talk with. He found a small stick and began tapping it on the ground. My dad said, "Look at me in the eyes and tell me, am I telling the truth?" My dad repeated himself. "You are telling the truth," is what A. H. said. My dad and A. H. were talking Cheyenne, and I explained to the other men what my dad and A. H. were saying. Then I said that now that we know the truth about these things, then now we need a new Arrow Keeper.[5] The men behind A. H. all agreed; they all nodded their heads. The conviction was clear, and the things he was doing were true, so the next process was to go after the Arrows.[6]

Somebody called from the Northern Cheyenne reservation and said that men are coming down on the twenty-ninth to

4. Laws regarding those who are directly involved in the care of the bundle of Mahoz, the Sacred Arrows, the holiest objects of Cheyenne religion, are restrictive and severe. The Arrow Keeper's behavior and actions inside and away from the Maheoneom, the Arrow Tipi, are tightly regulated. Violations of these laws are punished, and can result in the dismissal of the Arrow Keeper.

5. Mahoz are a gift from Maheo, the Supreme Being, and represent a covenant between him and the Cheyenne people. They are tribal property and belong to no individual or family. Keepers of Mahoz are selected because of their character and their willingness to devote their lives to the service of the holy objects. Through the centuries of their presence among the Cheyenne, Mahoz have gone from Keeper to Keeper. Some Keepers serve only four years, and others until their deaths. Because the Keeper is the highest spiritual leader in the tribe, his total immersion in his office is required.

6. The removal of an Arrow Keeper and the selection of another is a most serious affair and is preceded by ancient and secret procedures.

pick up the Arrows because the person who was there with
A. H., S. A., told the Northern Cheyenne that if there was any
better time to come after the Arrows, now was the time,
because A. H. was drinking right now. So the Northern
Cheyenne were coming down. So within this time period, we
had to have four meetings. So we put up four meetings and
went through the procedures. This was always stressed, that
we go through the procedures. So the fourth meeting we had
at R. Y.'s house. The men started congregating over there.
There were some men that couldn't be there because they had
to go to work, but they told us that they were behind us, and
there were some others that couldn't be there because they
were related to some of the others. Some called in, like L. T.;
he couldn't go because he was related to A. H. So we had a
meeting. There were about twenty-eight men. So we had a
meeting inside, and the vote was to ask the men what they
wanted to do. Should we go over there to protect A. H. to keep
the Northern Cheyenne from taking the Arrows, or do we
need to go over there and get them? So the vote was that we
need to go over and get the Arrows. We voted three times,
and all three times they came back and said we should go and
get the Arrows. We knew that if we did this, the police would
be involved. We went outside, and I had to follow a procedure that I needed to protect these men. We had a fire out
there, and I did what I was supposed to do with these men. I
painted all of the men. Then I asked, "Who wants to lead
this?" R. Y. came walking up towards me and said that he
thought I should. I agreed. I got in the pickup with my boys
and my brothers, and we took off. We pulled in front of A. H.'s
house. In the Cheyenne way, where the Arrow Tipi sits is his
property no more.[7] We have the right to go into the Tipi and
ask for a blessing.

7. The patch of ground on which the Arrow Tipi stands becomes tribal
property and remains so for as long as it stands there; when the Arrow Tipi
is moved elsewhere, its previous location returns to individual ownership.

I was never in the front; I was always behind. Only when danger came to my dad or my grandpa, then I went in the front. We pulled into his place. Edwards and I got the gifts and the money. We went up to the house. His wife was sweeping. She told A. H. to come to the door. He came on out, and I told him in Cheyenne what we had come for, that we had come for the Arrows. I got the basket, and I started to put it onto the concrete floor. He told me in Cheyenne to put it on the ground. This was the procedure. When he told me that, he agreed. Edwards and I put the things on the ground, and we explained what the things were for. We said fully everything in Cheyenne. I'm not going to review these words because they are important words that Arrow Priests are supposed to know, and I have these words today. He accepted the gifts: grocery baskets, blankets, shawls. For appreciation of what he had done before to try to help.

Once he accepted the gifts, then I called the men to come follow: Edwards Red Hat, L. B., Bryan Red Hat, Rondeau, C. Y., and the two other boys. They followed me around A. H.'s house. I told them how to take the pegs out, and they followed the procedure. Before we removed the pegs, we went in and untied the Arrows. We brought them out, and I told L. B. to sit on the ground and gave him the Arrows. Then we followed the procedures on taking the Tipi down. One man came from the front and told us to hurry, that A. H. had called the cops and that they were coming, and he went back. A few minutes later, another man came back and told us to hurry. I said that we had to follow the procedures. We continued on. Then R. Y. came and said we have to get going because the police are coming; they have guns and they're not going to back down. I had been praying all of the time we were doing these procedures. Eventually we got everything, and then another man came, and said we have to go. In the meantime, J. H. [A. H.'s wife] came and yelled at everyone. These boys were listening to J. H., and I told them to do what they were supposed to be doing. They went back to work. "Tell L. C. to back up," I said. L. C. didn't want to back up on his property. L. B. and L. C. drove off with the Arrows, and we continued to do the procedure. Me, Edwards, Steve, Rondeau, Bryan, F., J. and the other brother were the only ones there. I told L. B. they would have to stop four times to pray.

We finally left, and they had already been gone for about twenty minutes. All this time we kept praying that the police should not interfere. So I finally caught up with them, and there was one sheriff there, the Longdale sheriff, and he had stopped them. He had his light on. He told them that Concho [the Cheyenne-Arapaho agency] wanted them to stop, and that they had to wait there and not do anything. So when I came and pulled up, I got out of the pickup and started walking towards the sheriff. And all the men got off, and we all got around the sheriff's car. We talked for a moment, and then I said, "Jimmy, do you know Public Law 95–341? I think that means that you can't enter into any Indian affairs going on." Jimmy said, "No, I'm not; no, I'm not." Then Edwards said, "Okay, Jimmy, well, if you're not interfering, then we're going over to the house, and we'll be over there so you can come over there." And Jimmy said, "Okay, go on." So we got by, and then the first one came in, and my pickup was the last one coming in. They stopped by L. B.'s house. L. B. and L. C. started taking the Arrows. When I was coming over there, the first one I saw was Mainoma [Bill's sister]. These women were all standing in a line, and Mainoma ran up and said, "We knew you got the Arrows. We knew you were coming." And I said, "How did you know that?" She said, "We heard it on the scanner." She said, "They saw you in Enid, they saw you on I-240 south, then coming out of Weatherford and coming into Clinton, and then on Broadway in Longdale." Well, there is no Broadway in Longdale, but that's where we were sighted. We were sighted in those places. Anyway, we got here, and then they started telling the story. The cops came later, and we went out there and told them we were doing a Cheyenne procedure and that they had no business in this. To me it was like a miracle because they sighted us in those places; they saw us everyplace else but where we actually were.

The process was done. The procedures were followed. A. H.'s conviction that he said he was doing those things started it. The Arrow Keeper can do certain things, but he cannot do some things.

All of these things fell into place. There was a big miracle here, and that kept all of the men safe; and the procedures that were followed, by maintaining them and following them, that's what caused all of this action. Had we forgotten the procedures, we probably wouldn't have been successful. So that's it. The next day the police came again, and they tried to get the Arrows. They came four times. [Bill's father, Wayne Red Hat, became Arrow Keeper at this time.]

The thing is that previously I became an Arrow Priest and I went through the Arrow Ceremony.[8] They told me about these things that you have to observe, and that you have to watch these men do these things. I didn't know that these things have to go a certain way, and I watched them, how they went. The biggest part was that I could understand Cheyenne and I could talk Cheyenne. That's important. That's the main thing. So these guys that were older than me, some could speak Cheyenne but not as good, and some couldn't speak Cheyenne at all. And some of them went through the ceremonies, but that doesn't mean that gives them the right. What

8. The Arrow Ceremony takes place in a tipi considered a replica of the spirit lodge that stands inside the Sacred Mountain—Nowahwus, or Bear Butte, in South Dakota. On the fourth day of the secret ceremony, Mahoz are tied to a pole and are taken outside for Cheyennes to see and pay homage to. Because of their destructive power, only men are allowed to view the Arrows.

gives you the right is when you understand, when you look at things and you understand the whole mechanism of that one thing. You watch it, look at it, see what they're doing, how they do it, and then you go on to the next one because the next one does his ceremony, and the next one does his ceremony, and so on, all the way until it's through. And so by understanding all of that, and then I had two great big dictionaries, my grandpa and my grandma, so it was easy for me because I could go to my grandpa and ask him about something. And that's what I had on my side was that my grandma spoke Cheyenne to me when I was born, and my grandpa, and that was the main thing that these old people did for me by explaining these things.

My grandmother's grandfather was also Arrow Keeper.[9] It is interesting how I have different bloodlines through the Arrows. On my mother's side was Baldwin Twins, and then on my grandma's side was all the way back to Stone Forehead.

When the white man came and did the Indian Reorganization Act, I did some research, and I found out that in 1908 they sent a delegation to Carlisle or where the Cheyenne and Arapaho were going to school, and they asked the higher grades to draft up a form that the Cheyenne would follow. So they drafted up the rules and regulations of the chiefs, and what they did. They had the Arrow Keeper's rules and regulations, and when they drafted this paper up, the white men put his chiefs in there. It's basically what they're going to do in Iraq. They are going to say that they don't have a hand in it, but they do. That's basically what I found out is that they're actually destroying all of these ways.

9. Bill Red Hat's grandfather and father were Arrow Keepers. He traces his ancestry to Little Man and Baldwin Twins, who were Keepers during the early twentieth century. Bill is also the great-great-great-grandson of Stone Forehead, the Arrow Keeper who smoked the pipe with Custer seven years before the Battle of the Little Big Horn.

So anyway, by understanding these things, and then by going through these ceremonies, being in the Blue Sky before I became an Arrow Priest and helping my grandpa out, learning these sequences, that's the only thing I could do.[10]

The Blue Sky goes through the male line. Even though my Grandma Sophie had it for a while, it was because of my grandpa's dad, and when he passed away, she had all of the things that were in the house because she was with him at the time. Later she gave it back to my grandpa. So then when my grandpa became Arrow Keeper, he gave the Blue Sky to my dad. I was in the Blue Sky when I was fourteen years old, so I was already helping him do it at that time.

The Blue Sky is the making of this earth. The stars are in there. It wasn't really blue; it was glass because they used glass, but then as the beads came over and they were a pretty color, blue, then they started using the beads. But before, it was glass from lightning and from the rocks in the mountains.[11] The Blue Sky is made before the Arrow Ceremony. So it has to be made because you have to have the medicine to even touch the Arrows. So they bring the medicine from the Blue Sky Tipi.

The Blue Sky gives the people protection to go through what they need to do in the Arrow Ceremony unharmed because they are protected by the Blue Sky.

Knowing these things, these rules and regulations, the sequence of things, talking Cheyenne and understanding Cheyenne, being scared, you know Maheo is backing you.[12]

10. The Blue Sky bundle has been in the Red Hat family for generations. The Blue Sky Ceremony precedes the Arrow Ceremony and is an essential part of it.

11. The glass from lightning is called fulgarite.

12. Maheo is the term for the Supreme Being in the Cheyenne language. He created emamanstoon, "all the world," and gave it the order, vonoom, that has informed the ancient Cheyenne world description. The blue color of the sky visually represents Maheo. From him emanates the cosmic power, exhastoz, that permeates and maintains the world.

You can't see him. It tests your faith. You have to believe what you went through and what you learned, and then you can make it.

A lot of this whole thing is courtesy. It's about courtesy being with other men, and not making them feel low. Because at one point after I brushed them off and did what I was supposed to do, and I prayed for them, and then I asked them, "Okay, which one of you is going to lead this?"[13] So you give them that opportunity. You're not bullying your way through. You are giving all of these people this opportunity even though you know some things. You have to be courteous. So by asking them, the chiefs and headsmen of societies, that's actually where a lot of my power comes from, by being courteous to somebody. That's where all of my power comes from. That's what clears out a lot of animosity, hatred, meanness, madness, jealousy, but being scared never leaves anybody. Everybody gets scared, but you go and do it. That's what the soldiers say. There are bullets, and you can get hit and you can get torn apart, but you're going to do it. You don't want it, but by giving courtesy and following rules and regulations, you don't have any problem. So that's what I basically did. I gave other people things to do that were important. It wasn't me doing the whole thing, just the main parts so they don't make mistakes.

You have to know these things and believe in what you're doing, because it's hard to believe something when you can't see it. You have to keep that there. Sure you go down hills and everything and feel low sometimes, but it's part of knowing this whole thing.

---

13. A ceremonial man uses white male sage to "brush off" a person who has been in the presence of the sacred or death, thus returning him or her to a normal condition.

CHAPTER 3

"My Grandpa Taught Me about Being Worth Something"

April 11, 2003

As a small child out there in the blackjacks and going hunting with my grandpa, learning about these things—these plants, things like that—then going to school, Bible school, church, you still can learn all of these things. Many people aren't willing to struggle for it. Then they're out there and they run into the problems they run into, and there's not really anything you can do for them.

When I was small—about ten or eleven years old, you know, a long time ago—when they would bring groceries home, they brought them in crates, boxes, and the ends would be really thick, and thin in the middle. My grandpa made us shoeboxes out of these crates, and so we went to the filling stations and grocery stores and we stood there, me and Luther, and we had our shoeshine boxes and we got ten cents a shine. So we shined shoes. So I learned that. So by the time I was twelve, I was selling newspapers and cutting grass, and it was something that I learned. Then going to high school, I was the only one in this whole Canton area that had a project on pigs. I raised pigs for a while. Or hauling hay during the summer and then getting that done, and buying my own car by the time I was sixteen. I was getting paid two cents a bale. I gave half of my pay to my dad, but I still could buy a car. My grandpa taught me about being worth something; that was all learned from him. Then joining the service, and then getting money, and then even then giving some of the money to my dad to feed these kids here. Then after the service, I kind of went crazy for a couple of years. Then I worked for Beech Aircraft and then at Cessna, and then I went on to Boeing. I got good pay there. Then I met Nellie during that time, and then we just came back here because my grandpa needed me.[1] That's all he said, was that: "Grandson, I need you." Then when I got here, there were no jobs. But I worked out in the oil fields, as a roustabout. I bought my own truck and hauled hay. But you can do it. You have to have gumption. You have to have a lot of heart, a lot of endurance. Hauling hay is one hell of a job; it's a lot of work hauling hay.

---

1. "Nellie" is Nellie Red Hat, Bill's wife.

CHAPTER 4

"That's What I Think Has Gotten Me Here"

April 11, 2003

None of my kids were drinking or staying out late when they were thirteen or fourteen years old, or all through high school. I didn't start them in school until they were seven years old—because I knew that if I started them at seven, then they'll graduate at nineteen or twenty. And then they are wired together, and know what they're doing; they have more time to think. So by starting them out at the age of seven, by the time they were eighteen years old and their friends were telling them they could leave home, well, they didn't have that mentality because they were still in school. I always said to them, "When you graduate, then you can leave home." So by doing that, and then when they left home after that, I didn't have any problems with them because they could take care of themselves. But it was something I had to think about way back there when my first daughter was born, because I had seven years to think about this.[1] So

1. Bill's children are Marsha (Minni-ah-dah-le), Bryan (Van-hay-ohs), Luther Rondeau (Nah-ko-yo-eh-ne), Ona Sibyl (He-oh-ne-va), Emily Denise (Van-ha-y-oh), Eva Marlene (Si-ov-neh), Dorothy Mae (Hi-boh-he), and Minnie Mae (Mah-hah-ko-ah).

that's what I think has gotten me here: understanding the Cheyenne way and understanding this white man way, to where I don't get them confused but I can use them in their proper place.

I think I had a good upbringing with my grandpa, my grandma, and my mom and dad. It was a struggle. I mean, we didn't have everything, but we did have love and compassion for each other, and that was the most important thing.

The person that understands it all is the one who can protect all of the people. That's what he's saying [Bill's grandfather]. This is what I'm mainly saying on these tapes, is that I have to look at every situation to understand the cup that holds the whole body—that this thing, even though it's just a cup, it's a whole entity in itself. So by understanding it that way, you can understand what you have to say and what you have to do. It's also about not feeling bad if you don't know about something. Instead of saying, "Oh, no, I can't do it," that's what most people say, and that's where it hurts them.

It's about life situations. You go back and reference what happened a long time ago to help yourself, but it's about present day. They're not living back there. It's also about asking questions. This is part of my job. It's understanding today; it's not understanding when we had four hundred horses and how we are going to feed them and move the people to the next campground. I'm still from that time, but I'm using it today, and I have to live today, and we have to adapt to today. You always have to send somebody ahead to check the place out and see what it looks like.

CHAPTER 5

"People Need to See These Things"

April 11, 2003

My grandpa and my Grandpa Eddie had told me how to take a scalp.[1] I had the scalp in my pack. I got medevacked out of Antenna Valley. All of my stuff was in my pack. They probably found that scalp in there and threw it away. They had a scalp dance for me that night. But I lost it. They had a dance, put up chairs, had yard lights spread out. Dancers and singers came from all over that evening. Within a few hours when I came home from Oklahoma City, there was already a big group of people here. I was supposed to change my name, but I didn't want to. So I told my grandpa that. I killed an enemy, so you have to come back and tell it, so I told it. My grandmother, she used to be crying all the time. She would

---

1. The taking of enemy scalps was part of an ancient warrior tradition among North American tribes (Garbarino 421). On the deepest level of perception, the scalp meant that the dead person could not be reborn as long as that portion of his hair was in a stranger's hands. Although the custom was abolished in reservation times, Indian soldiers again took scalps in World Wars I and II and during the Korean and Vietnam wars. In doing so, these soldiers reestablished ceremonial features in their cultures that had been on the verge of extinction.

say, "My grandson is just eighteen, and he's having to see all of this." That really hurt her. The reality that she knew what I had to go through—that's what really got a hold of me. She really did care for me, that's what I got from that. And that she didn't want me to see those things. So there's a lot of heartache in all of that—a lot of bad things. I wish they would show the people they are killing, all the kids and everything. Let them see it. Let them hurray about it. Because this is what the government doesn't want to show the people. I think people need to see these things. The war won't have any effect if the people don't see these things. Then war is just going to be looked at as a great thing. The government says, no, don't show these things, because they're too graphic. But then they will always do what Bush wants, and the next president, they'll do what he wants. If they showed these things, it would make people think. It would put a shock into them that they'll think differently later on. It might not bother them now, but the next time something happens, they'll think about it.

CHAPTER 6

"All of This Has to Be Learned"

April 11, 2003

Just because you're Cheyenne, that doesn't instill you in a place. You have to earn it, you have to go through with it. It's a really hard way to let people down and tell them that they need to start from the beginning. My boys, they started a long time ago, so by the time Bryan was fifteen and Rondeau was fourteen, they made the Blue Sky. I had been teaching them years before. Man, I was walking on eggshells. They came up to me and told me that they wanted to do that. So I said, "Okay, I'll stay out of it. But I'm going to sit over there and smoke my pipe, and I'm going to pray." And then I sat there, and then I lay down and sat up again. And then I heard Bryan call me, and I walked to the tipi, and he told me that it made. So they made it the first time. But I mean, that's what it takes. They have to start from way back here, and with that it's really something. Starting from the beginning. So they can do it. It's a hard path. I've been really happy about what they have been able to accomplish.

All of this has to be learned.[1] You have to be in ear reach of what's being said. I've noticed in my situations that I know

---

1. There is a great emphasis on learning in Cheyenne traditional culture. The supreme teacher is Maheo, who taught the prophet, Motseyoef, who in

there were words I couldn't figure out. I knew something, but I didn't quite know what it was; but by thinking about it and praying about it, I remembered that my dad had told me something. I couldn't think of it at first, then all of it came back all of a sudden. I think in life, a situation has to be kind of drastic in order to trigger this, to turn it on. And it goes right to the right part.

Sometimes before, I used to struggle with things: "What am I going to do, what do I have to say, what do I have to figure out, what do I have to put down, how do I have to write it, how do I have to say it?" And then now, I just don't even worry about it. I just think, well, it's going to come whenever it comes.

---

turn taught the ceremonial people. All Cheyenne ceremonies were taught either by Maheo or by spirits on his behalf. All Cheyenne cultural features were taught by instructors from the spirit world. The place from which many Cheyenne religious and social features originate is Bear Butte: Nowahwus, "Where People are Taught." To this day, Cheyennes continue to go to Bear Butte on four-day fasts, seeking instruction from the spirits. They are initiated into the religious and military systems step by step, advancing slowly from one level to the next, and eventually, after many years, they master much of the complexity of the culture. Those who learned much and sacrificed much for knowledge were revered and regarded as the keepers of the tribal tradition.

CHAPTER 7

"And Then Everyone Was Gone"

April 11, 2003

My grandma told the story about Sand Creek. Her mother's aunt was at Sand Creek. Her name was Red Dust Woman. She told the story. She was seven years old when that happened. All that she remembered was that someone went hollering through the camp, and everyone was running, and she got lost or something in the crowd. So she just ran up to a man and woman who were putting these kids on a horse. She ran up to the woman and said, "Auntie, where do we go?" That was just a woman that was there in the camp. "Auntie, auntie, where are we going to go?" So she put her on the horse, and so two or three of them took off on the horse. The woman dumped them off in the brush outside of the camp, and then she rode back into the camp for more. She said she was watching the soldiers shoot, and she was watching that all happening. And then everyone was gone. They were watching it. There were people laying all over the ground; some people were still moving. And she was crying when she was telling this story. And my grandma used to tell me, toward the end she saw these Arapaho women coming in on horses, and these Arapaho women cut these Cheyenne women, cut their throats. She saw that happen. I never understood why they did that. I guess these Arapahos were what they called "hanging-around-the-fort Indians." They helped the soldiers. They probably wanted to eat; they were a small group, and the soldiers fed them.

CHAPTER 8

"This Is How We Know That You Are Cheyenne"

April 11, 2003

This one man had invited my grandpa and several other Southern Cheyenne to come, and he was going to tell a story, somewhere in Montana. So they came and they ate, and then after they got through eating, they went to another room. And this old man said, "I'm going to tell this story." So he covered all his windows and closed the door, and he started talking about this story. He was Hidatsa.[1] He was telling this story; he said, "This is how we know that you are Cheyenne. And the Cheyenne were somewhere way out there [motioning to the sky]. There was an arrow floating along, and it would come this way, sideways, come backwards, every way, upside down, just traveling, going in every direction, and finally it came to this place. And finally when it came close to the ground, it pointed itself straight down so it went

1. The Hidatsa tribe is from the Middle Missouri in North Dakota. The Hidatsas were friendly neighbors of the Cheyennes from the 1600s to the 1860s. See Jablow; Grinnell, "The Cheyenne Indians"; or Berthrong, *The Southern Cheyennes,* for a larger discussion of the relationship between the Hidatsas and the Cheyennes.

into the ground. The arrow was trying to come out. It was singing. While it was doing that, a grassfire happened. So this arrow was trying to pull itself back out of the ground, and the grassfire came and it burned the feathers. So eventually it came out after the fire, and it came out and it became you, the Cheyenne. We know you as 'Charred arrow feathers.' This is how our tribe knows you." He told that story, and it's two tapes long.

It's interesting because the story is based in the Cheyenne's own story.

CHAPTER 9

"You Have to Be Living It"

April 12, 2003

Some days I am just tired, and I just lie down and go to sleep. It bothers me and bothers me. People don't want to die; they want to live. And so you go through that and you take tumbles with them, and you go to the bottom, and you wonder why this thing can't be done right now. But I think there's a reason for that. It's to keep Maheo from being less big. And I'm learning that because I think it's a part of that—it keeps me humble. But I can see some things right now that are almost frivolous sometimes, and I can't understand it. Sometimes it almost seems frivolous, but they get out of it, whatever it was that was bothering them, or sometimes it sends them into the direction they need to go and get that done. But it takes time, and so what you see is that the Arrow Keeper is right there at that time. And then the next one comes in, and then you have to put this one to the side. And you have to try and see what these guys are saying, and your mind keeps going back to this one, but you have to try to do something for this next one. And that's where you have to really concentrate on asking for your help, because this is maybe sometimes too much. You are trying to separate, but you have to keep everything so you can see it.

It takes a toll on you, and I really do feel it. The only way I can get rid of that is when I throw up. That's when I know I can let it go and go on. It's like going into war, where people throw up. All that adrenaline and all of the chemical things coming from your brain and going into your body and making things go crazy, and then all at once you throw up, and then you're all right. I've seen this. Luther, my brother, he made a vow to go through the Arrow Ceremony.[1] And then we came out and we were all standing around, and this guy brought something to me and asked me to brush his wife off; she was having headaches. And then I knew right there, there was something else different, so I turned around and said, "Luther, come over here." And I put the gifts in front of him, and I said, "I want you to talk to her." Then when I put the gifts down, he doctored her. He can touch her while he's got this vow on, so he touches her head and starts praying that whatever's happening to her, that it goes away. But he doesn't realize, because this is his first time, he doesn't realize what's going on. Because as soon as she turns away to walk away after he finishes praying for her, and while he is trying to reach down to brush the gifts off that she gave him, he starts throwing up, you know, that cough. I could see it. I started calling to these guys, "Look, look, watch!" You're not going to see transfer.[2] But he starts throwing up, and he says, "Something's happening to me; I'm getting sick." And I said, "No, that's okay, throw it up, throw it up, go ahead." Because then you're taking all of that back out. So they came, and I

1. Each of the Cheyenne great ceremonies, Oxheheom and Maxhoetonstov, requires a male pledger who reenacts the origin story of how the gift of the ceremony was received. The Oxheheom also requires a female pledger who plays the role of the Sacred Woman at the time of the original granting.

2. Healing with power granted by the spirits usually transfers sickness from the patient to the healer. There is a process by which the healer is able to cleanse himself/herself.

explained that to them [the man and woman], and so they felt pretty good about it. But it just happens. Some of these things happen.

I think my main danger was that I kept thinking about it. I kept thinking about this one, and the one before and the one before, when I should have just let it go. And when I threw up, I should have realized that that's taken care of, because whatever they gave me to do for them is gone now. So it's not on them anymore. So these things are really—I mean, you really have to try to understand them. Sometimes you don't, though, and that's really hard. Because it's always something different. And some of the things that I am understanding is that when somebody comes here, crying that they want to live a long time, and they ask me to talk to Maheo, and I'm pleading to Maheo to come and help them, and then they get up and leave and go straight to the Jiffy Trip and buy a bunch of candy and pop—if they're serious here, they need to be serious there; they need to leave that stuff alone, because that's what's killing them. This thing isn't going to help them if they're not sincere when they leave here. But then it's their doing; it's not mine. You want things to be right now. That's what we're supposed to be doing. We're supposed to be living it. It's like Chief Dan George said: "I'm living it." [laugh] You have to be living it. You can't just jump from A to Z and expect everything to be all right. You have to live it.

So it's hard; it's a hard life, it's a hard way, but you have to just keep on trying to keep your faith even though, oh, I tell you, it can knock you down. You know, like in the winter when I go in the Tipi, and it's cold and I have to build a fire and I have to cross my legs. If you don't get that fire hot enough, and if you pray for about an hour, because it's cold, then after I get through praying, I have to try to stretch my legs, try to move them around, and then I can stand up again. And then I come back in the house and Nellie has the stove going, and I say, "Put some more wood on the stove." And she's hot and she throws some blankets on top of me, and I go back to sleep for a while. But by ten o'clock, I'm ready to go again. But it takes its toll on you. It was really hard on my grandpa when he started, because he already had aches and pains, and I didn't have any aches and pains until after I got in there. The doctor asked me about that. He said, "What do you do?" I said, "Well, the first thing I do when I get up, I go to the Tipi and I sit down and pray sometimes for about two or three hours." In the winter I'm back in bed by seven or eight in the morning to get warmed up, but during the summer I'm there sometimes until five o'clock in the evening. Sometimes I don't even come out. I just keep praying, and then I go to sleep for a while, and then I get up and start praying again, and then I come out, and sometimes the sun is already going down. Especially during the summer, because you can just relax, and it's cool in the morning, and you really get into prayer.

I pray for everything, everybody. But the ones I don't pray for, I don't think I can do anything for them. Because you tried, you tried to pray, and you ask them that they just don't come and bother.

Arrow Keepers in the past, they had it harder than me. They were doing it during times of war sometimes, and there were really a lot of things going on; and they had their share of problems. I know that Arrow Keepers had to be warriors before they were something else.[3] And they had to take care of their people, and by taking care of their people they were chosen. Like, say, a senator, he goes out and gets money and gets elected, and then he does things for people. Well, in the Arrow Keeper's position, you go out and work, and really

---

3. It is ancient Cheyenne belief that only one who has experienced war and physical destruction will be able, as Arrow Keeper, to work for life, for the protection of his people, for the original animal world, and for the world at large.

there's no pay. You go all the way this way, but you're doing all of this work here, and then you're known by your deeds. Then you're chosen.

It's the same way with the headsmen of societies. They go to war first. He's a soldier, and then he makes this headsman position because he is doing it by example, not by telling people "Go and do it." He goes and does it, and what he does, well, they see what he does. First you are green; you just want to go out and fight, or you just want to go and protect your people, but you don't really know anything. You're only watching. If you don't really know anything, or if you're not paying attention, you're eliminated. Then you're not able to lead a people. So you have to concentrate on what you're doing, because you're a kid and you're allowed to be stupid. But then you have to leave stupidness and craziness back there, and then you have to go this way. And even then, you have to be mindful of things, you have to concentrate, in order to make the next one. If you can't do this part over here, then you're eliminated. You have to understand everything going this way. So all your deeds and all your work is back here coming this way. And people have seen you going through all of these things, and then they will say, "Well, he will be good to do this position." You see, even the women are doing the same thing. They're saying, "No, this man would be better." They're telling their husbands because they have seen what the man did. But you have a line of fruit salad on your chest by the time you get over here. It's not like being elected and being put in that position and then given money to help people.

These situations that arise are for specific reasons, because they take me back to my grandpa. Whether he knew he was going to bring me back home [from Vietnam] or not, that wasn't the point, but that was the main thing he was saying: "Not until my grandson comes home." So by him not knowing the whole situation, but by these other things outside the spiritual ways, they are the ones that kept him on track. I think it was like a pact that can't be broken by him or the spirits. I think they made that plain. "Okay, you cannot just bring one boy home," so you have to do what you have to do. In other words, you have to work with this situation to get to this next situation. You have to do all of the formalities in this situation, but he doesn't know. But in his learning and his way to this point, he had to figure out each situation. Whether they are right or wrong, they are getting him to this next point.

So it's just like an accident. Most people look at an accident as a bad thing, but yet at the same time it probably was a good thing, too. You can't stop the accident because you don't know if they're going to have an accident or not. But what you're saying is that you don't want them to have this accident, but that if they do, that they are able to work through to the next point. That's all you can do. So when my grandfather knew I was over in Vietnam, he couldn't be there. The only thing was to pray this way for me to get here at this other point. So that's the only thing I can do. I can't really—well, let's say I can drive to Montana. And I say, I'm going on this trip, I am going on this road, and I don't want any highway patrols on this road because I'm going seventy-five or eighty. And I have to believe that. And for some reason, at the top of the hill I just slow down and a highway patrol comes by. For some reason, there were no words saying I should take my foot off the gas; there's nothing like that. It's just that I slowed down for some reason, and then the highway patrol comes flying over. But he's still on the road. You asked for it to be clear. But for some reason it teaches you these things that makes you grasp these situations before they even happen. So by making that prayer, on a safe trip, like praying when you go back, "Help them to get home safely," but if there's an accident on the way, there's a reason for that, and then you pray that they're going to work through that. So when he was praying that no harm come to me, and then I turn around and get wounded, that's what he has to figure out. So by him figuring it out and saying what he had to say, we all came home.

What I'm looking at more now: I know that they might go across there [to Iraq]. I also want them to be able to come out of the Gulf War Syndrome and not let that bother them if they have to do that. It's a tough situation, but these things have to happen sometimes. I look at when the soldiers attacked. But I can understand now why they attacked the women and children. It's because they couldn't fight the societies [Cheyenne soldier societies] on their own. So the next best thing is to go and kill the people, and this brings the societies to their knees, and then they turn around and give up. It's like a bird on her nest—how she runs away with her wing hanging down like it's flopping. And she's flopping it, and she knows what she's doing, but that's natural; I mean, it doesn't come natural to us. Her instinct, or whatever it is, tells her to run away, get caught over here, and then your babies will be okay. So a lot of this is, the way I understand it, a lot of these things that we know as animal-type ways, that's what were the teachers in the beginning. These animals themselves, they were here first, and we have to learn from them, we have to learn from the ones who were here first.[4] So you learn from these animals.

A good example is this guy was going to be a medicine man, but he didn't know how to treat some wounds. But he knew a lot about roots, so one of his intelligent ways of chemistry was to shoot the bear in the stomach with an arrow and then follow the bear with the stomach wound to see what he ate. So the guy followed the bear to see if he was going to die. Well, if he died, then the chemistry test went up in smoke.

4. In the Cheyenne creation story, Maheo created animals before he created humans. Thus, animals became important early teachers for the people.

But if the bear lived, eating so many of these things, the guy learned, he learned through that.

I always think about this turtle. We use this turtle. This turtle can go underground for six to seven months—it depends on the weather—and he can slow his heartbeat down. It's the same way with this lizard. But if this person is going to follow these ways, he has to follow the animal and see how he is going to do it, and constantly ask him to be shown in that direction, in that area. So maybe there were some people that knew what the lizard could do that was important today to this medicine man who was still alive. If this cancer was growing in this person, the medicine man could go and tell the person, "Okay, do this, do this shallow breathing," and therefore the cancer can't eat what it's supposed to live on, and he would give him certain things that would be helpful to the person. So that's what he learns coming this way. So that's what I think about with fever. A long time ago, they would cover us up, we would sweat it out, and the fever would go away. That's what my grandmother did for me all the time, but now it's medicine to cool the person down. But I don't think it works that way; I think it needs to go back to the original thing. If you went back to the original thing and killed the fever, whatever was in there was gone. But now you're taking medicine, and the fever is lingering and it's festering, it's doing something. It's not balanced with its host that's carrying it. So this person gets sicker and sicker.

So that's what I think about these ways; that's what they tell us. We have the bear, we have the buffalo, we have the coyote, we have the wolf, we have the eagle, the badger; in Cheyenne, we have all of these animals inside of this Tipi.[5]

5. Mahoz protect not only the Cheyenne people but also the world order as created by Maheo. Of special concern are animal species threatened with extinction. They are spiritually and physically represented in the Arrow Tipi.

All of these animals are put in there for a specific reason, because the white man put a bounty on all of these things. Now, if we didn't do that, white men would be successful in killing all of them. They would kill them all. Then our ceremony would disintegrate because we don't have these animals anymore. So by us continuing to have these things inside this Tipi, they are still alive. So he can bounty on the buffalo again, and he might get pretty close to killing it again, but they still continue. But they are already there. We can't take these things out. We have to leave them in there. Always. So they are under the protection of that. I guess if we would have had the dodo bird in there, it would still be alive, too [laugh]. I don't know, we don't have it. But there is a reason for all of these things. I mean, it's not just something that survived on its own. It's about helping each other.

I think the biggest part of our downfall is going to be our language. You really have to look at the big picture; it's not just one thing.

The animals give us our language. I can't really decipher it for you, but it's through them. We were what they referred to us. They called us "hearing ears people"; that's the way they understood us, that's how they knew who we were. So these animals have names for us, too. So as long as they use them and as long as we use them, then we're okay. We cover each other's base. So there are a lot to these things. It's understanding all of these things and using them and asking for some of these things that we don't know. Before we went to get the Arrows, there were rabbits and birds that were just kind of coming to where we were doing something; they were just kind of coming. I remember one day we were sitting out there, and they always told me that when you pray, and if you're praying right, well, the chickadee comes, and he listens to your prayer and takes off with it and goes to give it to the next person. The same way with these humming-birds; it's the same thing. They come to listen to what you're doing, and this hummingbird came flying in, and it was going to land right here on the sweat lodge I was sitting by. Instead he came and landed by my foot. And I've learned to understand now. But when I saw the hummingbird, it was sitting there on the ground, on the grass, looking up at me. So what I had to do was remember my sentence before he landed there and during the time he was there, and the sentence afterwards. And then when I learned that and understood the sentences, this is what he was telling me: "Hey, you're telling the truth here." But if he wasn't there, I was talking out of my head.

I told a lot of these stories to some of these guys and explained it to them. And one of them was about to die and came to the camps last year and said, "You know, I had doubts about you, but everything you told me, it came; it came to the hospital and told me." So I have people out there that do that—they come and tell me and explain things to me that happened to them, and I just explain to them that when you need to ask me something and I tell you, if you want to do something, then all of your problems start. So I have to tell them that "All of your problems are going to start." I explain to them that just because they are here right now and think something is coming to them, they are asking for it, and they have to be aware of it wherever they are from that time on. If they aren't, then some problems might happen. You have to get back to your prayer, get back to your thinking. I just explain that to them: you have to keep on praying and keep on thinking honestly about these things, and you won't have these problems. But if you start to have these problems, then you're not thinking about what you said over here. They want to try to do things for themselves, but they're not in it like me.

One guy came and asked me, he said, "How do you know to help these people? These are all your people. Why don't you just go out there and tell them?" I can't. It's never done that way. You can't make somebody do something. They have to want to. So I explained to him when they want to, they come here, and then when I tell them, they want to learn. That's why they're here. But before, they don't want to learn. When they come here, then my job is easier. You can't drag them off the street and say, "Hey, you need to behave, you need to think this way." I can't really do that. That's not my place. It's them. Part of my job is waiting on them.

I had a biker come out here. He had tattoos all over his arms, big arms [laugh]. He's married to an Indian woman over there, and he said she's doing something to him. And I sat down and talked with him and said, "What is it?" So he explains everything what he thinks is happening to him. And he's telling me he believes. But he doesn't believe, I mean. Then I turn around and tell him, "Okay, I'm going to give you this. You go, and if this doesn't happen, then you come back, and then I'll give you this. And if you come back on the fourth time, that means that you're telling me a lie, you're not believing what you're telling me—you don't want that belief to go with you. So then you come to me, I'll go get rid of it." Usually they don't come back because they get their belief, and that's what gets them to go through it, whatever their problem was. But all I did was give them Linus's blanket. I mean, he's a white guy [laugh]. They don't believe in these medicines and everything, but you know, that's what you have to do—you have to get inside his head. He came back three times, and then he didn't come back. So everything's all right with him. But then he didn't want to be a liar in front of me, maybe, or maybe he was really wanting to do something to help himself. So in that instance I just pointed things out for him that he needed to concentrate on.

I've had all kinds of white guys and white women out here that come and ask. It's not just Indians that come here. It's something that you have to explain to them. Like I told you about the dream already—it's their dream, it's not my dream. All I do is bring it out for them by just asking them questions. Sometimes it's a psychological thing. Some people are just psychologically hurting; they're not really hurting at all. You know, you have all kinds of people like that, that don't really have any problem, and all you need to do is just put them in the right direction. So you try the best way to help them. And so by telling this guy you don't have enough faith—he never did want to be told that, I think, but still I had to tell him that, because there was really nothing I could do for him that he would understand. So the only thing was just to listen to what he was saying and working on what he was saying, so when he left, why, he was all right. He actually brought me a great big ol' sword [laugh] on the third time that he came. Some other white guys that come and want help, you just sit there and listen to them, to what they have to say, and you get them in their belief. They want to have belief. But that's all it takes, is to kind of nudge them in that direction, and then once he believes in himself, he can do a lot of things on his own.

Now, there are times when you do really need prayer, when you're really sick or something; then you really have to do some things. There were these ones that came, they were contemporary Indians, Cheyenne boys, that live over there, and there is this thing, spirits, coming out of a hollow tree that went way down into the earth and would come out so many times and scare them. And they viewed this thing as powerful, and it was bothering them, and so I had to try to figure out what they were doing, what it's all about, because they are not really into what I'm doing. They're not talking Cheyenne, so they can't understand what I'm saying here. So you have to bring something, Linus's blanket—you have to bring something and give it to them. You know it's a crutch that you give to them; everybody knows that. We don't think about it. We don't use it in our daily life. So I gave them something. But then you give them enough strength to go and do something, and they can take care of it themselves. They can get well on their own.

So some of these things are psychological. Some say I am a good psychologist. But it's knowing these things. I can't clear the way for you, from all the accidents that you might have in the future, if there are going to be any, but I can prepare you for them. Because when you do come into them, then things, if you're understanding, then whatever you run into, you'll be able to go over, or go around, or go through. It's the same thing that my grandpa was doing for me over there. He couldn't go over there to help me. The only thing he could do was pray over here, for me to understand what I needed to do to protect myself, to be more mindful of what's going on. That's virtually one of the main things; if you're mindful, then you don't have as many problems.

It's Maheo's doing, and so I'm just doing what he's been saying, and I've been doing what my grandpa's been saying: "Grandson, you have to believe." And then when he died, something happened to me. And then your dad dies, and he tells you the same thing: "Believe." And your grandma dies, and she keeps telling you the same thing: "Believe." So there's something to this belief, because when they're dying, it's hard to fathom that sometimes. But you have to try to understand it. I didn't know some of these things, but it's like, when you lose somebody, that's where you learn. Because then your guts, then everything's all out. You're just vulnerable to anything. But then you either go deeper in your prayer or you go higher in your prayer, whatever. You keep on, because what happened is that they left you wide open, but then you are better adapted to catch on, to fathom what's happening. You don't understand in the beginning. You are all of the emotions that come out, all of the bad things that come out. You're mad, but that's all a part of learning this whole situation. And then you realize that what they were saying is that "Grandson, you have to believe." Because they have believed this far. So you have to take that and run with it. It's hard not knowing the right thing, but you have to believe that it's the truth that they're telling.

The Arrow Keeper's job is to try to understand; that's what it means, "understand everything." I will sometimes make the point to some of them. I tell them, "Okay, what is this?" [He points to a coffee cup.] Everybody will say, "Cup." And then they leave it at that. But the main thing about this thing is that this body is held in something. Without this cup holding us, we would be fluid like that [pointing inside the cup]. But they're not understanding it that way. They're saying, "It's a coffee cup, you drink from it." But they're not understanding that this body is also the same thing, it's also this cup. They're not really understanding what it is. It comes from the stars. That's the word, it comes from the stars. The stars, they are contained in something. But it's so vast that you can't fathom it. So most people can't fathom that this is a container that holds their body, their life, but they're not looking at it like that. So they're not really thinking. And all you have to do is just try to get them to think what you're thinking, because you've been through a lot of this undecisiveness. Anyway, that's how I understand it. That's the way it was told to me, so that's why I'm telling it to you. So there's really nothing I can say and do unless he's listening. I have to say and do it right before he listens. If I don't do it right, then he's not listening. It's real hard to figure it out.

CHAPTER 10

"The Main Thing Is to Hang on to Your Ways"

April 12, 2003

All of these present-day things are learned from way back there. We were the hunted way back then.

When Sweet Medicine came, he put order in our lives.[1]

It reminds me of a story, what happened to my grandpa. It's about seven or eight miles to Canton, where they used to live. It's underwater now, on the north side of the lake. He used to go to work for the county. At that time, he was getting something like seventy-five cents a day. So he would walk all that way to Canton. He would go to work and come home. They still had Indian things that they wore back then. I guess my grandma had a dress, you know, buckskin and beaded and everything. And one time they needed some money, and so they hocked it to buy food, or whatever they had to have. So one day he went to work and he was getting paid, and my grandma told him to be sure to get the dress out

---

1. Sweet Medicine, Motseyoef, is the Cheyenne prophet, born from a girl who was conceived from a star. He brought the gift of Mahoz from Nowahwus and initiated the Cheyenne military and political systems and taught the Cheyenne code of law.

after you get paid. So he did, and, well, Oklahoma weather can change on you just like that. So anyway, he was on his way home and it started to blizzard, it started snowing. He was having a hard time, and late at night he got so tired that he lay down and he laid inside the dress. He put the dress on, and that more or less saved his life. Because when he woke up in the morning, he heard two people talking about him, and one was wanting to take him because that one said he was dead. But the other one said, "Well, maybe he's still alive. I think he's breathing; you can't take him." So they were kind of arguing with each other, and my grandpa was just listening. Pretty soon he finally started moving to see who was talking about him. So he got up to look around, and there were no footprints out there. And so he walked on home. He got into the dress, he crawled into the dress.

It reminds me of the word we use for the buffalo: we call it "Issiwun." A long time ago, there were hunters that used to get caught out in the snow or blizzard and couldn't do anything, so they would kill a buffalo, take the insides out, and get inside, and this kind of more or less saved their lives. So this is what I understand Issiwun to be. It was something powerful. It wasn't like money, or anything like that that we think about today. It was something powerful that's really there that's going to help them, that's going to save their lives. Therefore, in ceremonies we call it Issiwun. It means "get inside."

I've learned to understand these words and try to use them, but their meaning has its own explanation. Like this one my grandma told me: they call the quail, and it comes from the tune, what he's saying. So it's the same way with the crow; it's his word, his language. It's like they are naming themselves. The Cheyenne name for cougar, or puma, if you break it down, it's "killer, jump, horse," so they're actually killer of horses. So that's what his name is.

This story about the Great Race comes in, too: The road-runner, the eagle, the magpie, these things ran a race.[2] What they instilled for us is that it also gave them power. They raced—some say in the Black Hills area, some say Bear Butte, so it's another interpretation again. But still it's a race that they had to run, and they had to win. And a human couldn't do it, so he had to ask some things to help him—because he didn't want to be eaten by these animals. The humans were tired of being hunted; they implored the spirits and the powers that they didn't want to be hunted. So the spirits said, "Okay, then this is what you have to do." So they had to make some kinds of amends. So when the birds won, and won this thing for them, then it also gave them power, and so they are the ones that can eat animals, too. So every time I see one of these animals, I think it's good luck. They were running for the humans. The magpie won.

Then Maheo gives us Sweet Medicine, and he teaches all of these things. He showed us a lot of things.

The Sweet Medicine time, all of this time was utopia-like. I would think that that's the only way it could be, because Sweet Medicine is somebody powerful sent by Maheo to teach these guys something. And then so these guys learn this, and then they are carrying it. It's too much of a utopia because you are just focused on your group—you're not thinking about these others that are coming. He warned about that; he's told that. As long as you hold on to these things, you will have these things. But there's a time coming

2. When humans arrived in the world, their position was tenuous at first: Would they be hunters or would they be the hunted? The spirits organized a Great Race in which a human runner was pitched against the swiftest animals. The race was won by birds who sided with the humans. Today these birds (the magpie, golden eagle, and roadrunner) play important roles in Cheyenne religion. Cheyenne oral tradition places the location of the Great Race in South Dakota.

when this band we call earth man, coming on earth man, he's coming, and he's going to make a big change in your lives.[3] He is going to bring these things, and he's saying that you have to hang on, hang on to your holy ways. When the guns came over, we were told that we were to follow this way: Whatever is white, don't take it. So we didn't know, but processed flour, sugars, lard, all of these things are white. By him telling us that we shouldn't take these things, but these things, we couldn't get away from them—well, it becomes another way. Then it's survival after it gets to over here. It's just trying to stay alive because they have taken some of these things from the white man.

One of the taboos is that the Cheyenne are all afraid of owls. But that's not true. Because you have bowstrings that use owl feathers. But what they learned, what I'm saying, it's like a rag. I'm talking about a rag, but you have to understand what I mean about that rag. You have to try to put all of these things inside it. What I'm trying to say about these things, all of these things that are remnants, they killed all of our teachers, all of our scholars, people that knew how to do things, our professors. They killed all of them, and so all of this has changed us as Cheyenne. So I'm having to try to work with that, these remnants. Let's say there is a big story, and only this part got saved, and this part got saved, and then we're trying to piece that together: what did they mean, what did they say? A lot of these guys are lost. They don't have these stories from way back there, and they're picking up just these remnants.

They all will come together. Now we know what to do to reach out. It's like putting up a festival. You have to have all kinds of people that know different things, from cooking to

---

3. At the end of his life, Sweet Medicine prophesied the Cheyenne future. He predicted the arrival of an animal yet unknown (the horse) and the coming of bearded white men.

organizing to getting things done. Well, it's real because there are all of these different stories from these different people. We won't get together now because this is not the time and the point. It's going to wait for a time and a point to do this when things get pretty bad. I always kind of look at that as one story, too. I look at us Cheyenne still being here when they destroy a lot of other things.

The main thing is to hang on to your ways, and it's going to pull you through. It might look like water over there, but for some reason the ground is going to come out of the water, so that when devastation comes, you will be able to walk on the ground to this other place. The ground makes a bridge to travel across.

CHAPTER 11

"You Have to Serve and Then You Become"

May 2, 2003

At the time of this visit, a busload of representatives from the Texas legislature had driven into Oklahoma in an attempt to filibuster a vote initiated by the Republican faction. The vote was aimed at redistricting certain areas, which would benefit the Republicans. Bill, my father, and I talked about this news event, and the following narrative ensued.

In the course of our discussion, Bill mentioned oral history. Much of the vast body of Cheyenne oral tradition has been lost; however, a great many stories continue to be told throughout the Cheyenne community, and numerous stories have also been told to anthropologists and have been published. Important elements of oral tradition are alive and kept secret, revealed only in ceremonies or in the Arrow Tipi to a closed circle of participants.

SMS: What does oral history mean to the Cheyennes today?

BRH: Well, it works. Two weeks before my grandpa died, he called me into the front room, and he showed me his pipe; he showed me the one that Jack Wood House made for him one time a long time ago. And then he said, "I want you to have it." And me knowing how this thing works when someone starts giving things away, they instinctively already know something. Now, whether they are going to look at instinct as nothing, he gave me his pipe and he said, "You're going to have my medicine." And so other people are trying to say my grandpa didn't do that, and they tried to get the Arrows. So that right there shows it. And now they are using the white man analogy on the Indian Reorganization Act, that when the government picked chiefs, and they put them in these positions, and they said, "You are going to be representative of this or that," and they told them that they were chiefs, and some of them weren't chiefs, but they became chiefs through the government's eyes. Some of them were real chiefs, original chiefs.

One of the questions that was asked was what happens if this chief dies, for example, or doesn't want to continue to serve. Well, it was passed on to a successor, in the government's eyes. When the Indians turn around and read this thing, they assume that since he was chief, he can give it to his son or grandson. But that isn't the way that works. But this is the white man way. The law to be a chief is a real strict traditional way, and it involves holy things, whereas when this guy is going to be chief, he works all of his life, beginning when he's young, and then he becomes chief. But he has been serving his people all of this time. Now, that's the Cheyenne way. Now, the white man way—well, you know the white man way, how he does that, and then he serves his people. But he's being paid by somebody. That's not the Cheyenne way. In the Cheyenne way, you have to serve and then you become. Because then people see what you are doing, and they pick you on your merits, on your character, on your actions, how you handle yourself in the camp.

SMS: So do Cheyennes go along with this process today?

BRH: Some of them. But not all of them. Because they don't want to be chiefs like that. As long as you go over there and stick your hand out for a medallion, they'll give you one [laugh].

The thing is that these things are picked. They are picked through ancestry, and the ones who do this are the people that know these rules and regulations of how these people are picked, through his merits, not through his being picked and then serving the people. It doesn't work that way.

Even if some people say that the new way is the way it is supposed to go, I'm still here doing what I'm supposed to be doing, and so they can do whatever they want to do out there, but it doesn't affect this over here.[1]

When the government told them you can take this new way or you can remain with your traditional people, when they took this new way—see, these are C and A's [Cheyenne-Arapaho] now; they're not all Cheyenne—they picked this way, and now then that's the way the government's going. That's where they come and say, they tell us government-to-government relations. Well, I mean, that's what they are trying to do with these people out there. But these other people are trying to maintain their traditional way. And then they don't like that because they don't have any say-so. And the reason why they don't have any say-so is because there is no way some other man's analysis is going to come in on some tradition that's been going on for thousands of years. But then we're getting thinned out at the same time.

But the Cheyenne way is that when you give something, that's the way it is. You don't have to have any dignitaries

1. The world of the dominant society and the ancient Cheyenne world, as exemplified by the Arrow Tipi and the Great Ceremonies, have clashed from the beginning of Euro-American conquest to today. The Arrow Keeper and those who support him are continuing guardians of the ancient order.

there; you don't have to have fifteen different countries there. And everybody's sitting in their chairs signing papers and taking pictures and all of these things that you see that are supposed to be so dignified that, man, I tell you, it just runs over people. And then they turn around and say that they're there for the people. They're not there for the people.

The people's way is a lot better than any governmental structure or any capitalist structure, because in the long run you benefit more from it. You don't get rich from it, but you have all the knowledge, all of what makes you who you are. And as much money as they make, they can't buy it. They can't pay for it. That's why I like Khomeini, you know. He stood up for his rights, and he kicked all of the foreigners out. That's the way it's supposed to be. You're supposed to have embassies, I mean, people that go between; that's who you deal with. That's who tries to deal with them. Say, well, I'm sorry, these Cheyennes say no; it's not going to be worked that way—that's what they're going to say, it doesn't work that way. So they can go ahead and do what they're doing. All they're doing is just really, it's almost corrupting the people the way they are fighting about things. So that's the result of that. The government wants us to be capitalists. Okay, they make money, thieves, they steal money, so on and so forth. I mean, you can go on down the line. So our Cheyenne people are just what the government wanted. They know how to steal money, they know how to use the loopholes, they know how to use the gray areas, so what are they talking about?

This thing isn't going to work, the way they're doing it.

So, anyway, this oral way of doing things, it must have done something for us. I mean, I understand we had medicines and markings and everything, but the soldiers got rid of that and burned all of that. I saw a book about this school out east, Carlisle. There was a guy that wrote a letter to his family. And they say that one of the generals took the letter that was given to Howling Wolf. It was so simple. It showed some scaffolds. It showed three men that had a certain kind of headdress. It showed trails going to the man that died that the people respected. The one that died that the people respected had a lot of tracks around it. So it was telling them that this one was respected because many people came. And it was a good explanation, better than I am explaining now. So I mean they drew things and sent them to each other, but it wasn't the way we write a letter. It was pictures. I wish I could get that. I wish I could get all of that.

It wasn't like the way they have documents now. This oral history, the only way you are going to learn it is you have to be there. If you can't be there, you can't learn it. If you don't have the initiative or the drive, you don't need to be there anyway. So it works.

I think this oral history is going to be the only one standing, because the person with documents isn't going to be standing there. It's the ones who are talking to each other, telling each other what happened next or what's going on next. I mean, it automatically works if you think about it. You can't get the other side to believe that, but it does work. Because whenever something happens, there's talk, so everything gets told. Then the police come along and they want to do something, and then they mess it all up. They don't get it right because this guy is trying to think about what he said, what all happened, and he already told it. So anyway, it works.

So far, whatever I've done through oral history, through the Cheyenne way, I've been pretty lucky.

This way that somebody tells you and that—see, they don't look at the validity of this old man making this statement, and they don't really realize how he made these statements with Maheo and Motseyoef and these spirits. When he told them that he's not going to take the Arrows until his grandson comes home, that in itself is a hundred countries witnessing something, because that brought me back, and the others back, too. But they don't realize what that meant, what that means, and so even if we step aside and let them take them [the Arrows], they're still back here. We've re-proved and re-proved and re-proved ourselves. It's a hard thing.

It's about truth—Maheo's truth. It's not my truth; I'm just working through it. I've just been told this is the way you have to go. I mean, if you're not supposed to kill somebody, then you're just not supposed to do that. It's plain and simple, and then you can make rules for these other things, but the one that does the killing, he still suffers through this whole thing. I mean, just because you are on the winning side—just like I told the judge back there, "Just because all of you are the dominant society, that doesn't make it right." It doesn't make it right just because you pass a law about the D.A.R.E. program that this thing is going to be good, and everything is going to work.[2] You have people that are different ethnic backgrounds, and that means something. There are different ways, and the white man law doesn't connect with these other ways. It will run parallel from here to eternity, but it will never come together. So that's what I'm saying. This oral history is something that people don't try to realize.

It's what we know. That's what we're doing. That's how we're making this next thing. And then if we did it all wrong, they'll let us know when we get over there, and it will change back someplace down the road. But anyway, like I said, this oral history, this is the Cheyenne way. Tribal law supersedes C and A law, federal law, U.S. law. I know there are a bunch of people that would like to fight me on that [laugh], but I think I still would win.

It was real funny. I went into the court after I wrote this paper up, and I gave it to the judge. He looked at it. I told

2. D.A.R.E. (Drug Abuse Resistance Education) is a national anti-drug program sponsored by local police departments, which work with schools to teach students how to avoid drugs.

him, "I want that stamped" [laugh]. So he took it in there and had it stamped by the court clerk. So in their eyes it became an official document. Sometimes I feel bad because I don't have any money to go talk to a lawyer and get something done, and I just pray about it. And I really feel bad and I feel hurt. And then I go and finally eventually do something about it, and it turns out all right. But I don't know why I feel hurt so much about that. But eventually it turns out. Then on some things I just more or less let them go. I kind of feel that I should have done something, but at the time I didn't know what to do.

What I'm saying is that we have to re-prove ourselves again and again. We have to spend money when we could be buying something else. That's what makes me angry. The whole thing, the whole thing these people have to go through just to get their rights, or just to make people understand what they were told orally. It's a shame, because they could have used the money for something else, like for food or electricity or something. We just have to re-prove everything. Even like the judge over there. He wasn't going on my word alone, when a lot of them take my word. That made me angry.

Anyway, oral history is here, and it needs to be thought out.

It's about the white man wanting us to learn to be a white man, so they are learning how to cheat and steal, they're learning all of that, what the white man wants. Maybe one day they'll steal the land back from him [laugh].

Here's what I'm saying. Even though it looks bad, if he comes to me and we go do the right thing and he's telling the truth, there's nothing that's going to defeat us. If they don't come, I can't do anything for them. If they come, we help them. So that's the way it's been going. So even though you don't see a big building, a United Nations building, sitting here, but this thing has its authority and its power. It's so simple. But they're looking for magic bullets, and they're look-

ing for money, but if they say the things right, come here and
say the things right, they get what they need. So there are still
a lot of people that come. As long as they're telling the truth,
that's what it's all about. As long as they come to me and we
do the right thing in there, it comes about.

Oral history is always going to be here, and the white man
is always going to try to knock it out, because he has papers
that say you should do it this way, and then everything will
be fine and everybody knows. But that isn't what it's about;
it's not about everybody knowing. It's about people striving
to understand something. I mean, if you're going to go up a
mountain, you go all the way to the top, or you say, "Okay,
look, you go all the way to the top and you put my flag up
there, and you tell everybody that I went up there." I mean
[laugh], that guy might get it done, but it will make people
real mad, because that's not the way it's done. So you know,
it's just plain and simple. I don't know why people can't see
it. You have to go up the mountain yourself; you can't have
anybody else go and do it for you. So all the dangers and all
the things, the pitfalls, the cracks and crevasses that you're
going to try and make it over, that's what you have to try to
do. And if you're a person that is wise, or is becoming wise,
you're going to make it. But if you're not, you might slip and
fall and kill yourself, and you weren't meant to go up there
in the first place because you didn't have all of what it takes.

But that's what I'm saying about this thing, is that you
have to decide. If you love somebody that much, if you love
something, you are going to have to tell your wife, "Nellie,
we're going home because my grandpa wants me." And she
was living in an apartment and everything, and going to
work and everything, but that's the way it had to be. And so
all of the money I could have had, it's all here. So that money
wouldn't even really cover it if I had to have money to learn
about something. So by doing that and coming home, I mean
it was tiresome. Because Grandpa wanted me just to be here

and just to sit. Then when I got here there were no jobs, and I went to work welding and roustabouting and everything. You're dependent on that, and you have to go that way, so I just said, well, it's not the best job in the world, hauling hay, but you have to sacrifice and do something. Because then I could say, "Today Grandpa is having a meeting," shut my equipment down, and go to the meeting, or I could pay some other guys to go and finish up the field over here. I mean, that's just finding a resolve, understanding something. You don't like it, I didn't like it, man, but I used to like to smell the hay cut in the spring: "Ah, man, let's go and get our equipment ready." And then we started fixing tires and putting grease in things and moving them around and making sure they're going to work . . .

I'm finding that there's no problem that can't be solved. Anyway, hopefully these things will go on, and Bryan will know what to do. I trusted him at fifteen and Rondeau at fourteen. They went in there and made the Blue Sky together. I was sitting outside. Oh, man, I was just sitting there and praying, just wanted to help them somehow. But I mean, really, the kid knows what to do. It's just like you are always going to worry about your kids, but if you just let them go, they take care of things. That's another law, that it's going to be that way.

SMS: How do you see yourself in this long line of persons doing what you're doing?

BRH: I'm glad I'm here. And I know I have a big responsibility. And that when somebody comes, I just ask them to help them some way. What I feel sometimes is that I don't know enough. I mean, I make examples of that by that whatever Grandpa knew, and if my dad at least got half, that would be all right, and that whatever my dad knew, if I only got half of that. And I try to be lenient on myself at the same time, because maybe I didn't get that much, or maybe he didn't get that much, but still, it seems to be sufficient. Because I always take myself back to those ones at Sand Creek. What did they feel? I know they were hurt; I mean, I haven't been hurt like that. But I wonder about that. What was the Arrow Keeper thinking? What was going through his mind? And he has this thing here. And sometimes I feel like that. But then I look at all of the things they had to go through just getting here, and it was cold, and so I count my blessings. But we're still being attacked on every front; they are always trying to do something. They are always trying to change the [Cheyenne-Arapaho tribal] constitution so that they can come over here, so that the police can have an authority here, but it never panned out. I have the draft. The thing is that they try, though, and so we have to send people over there and spend money on this thing. It's always a fight on something that's so stupid. They don't have to have the authority over here.

I always wish we had a lot of things, but it sometimes doesn't work out that way. But actually, we get what we need.

Oh, man, sometimes I really think I'm alone. Sometimes I feel like I'm just sitting here. But I know I get a lot of help from other people. They come and tell me that they've been praying for me. But sometimes when you sit here by yourself, it goes into never-never land [laugh].

Where did we start this one?

[I remind him about the Texas legislature going into Oklahoma, finding the loopholes, how people find the gray areas.]

BRH: That's why you have lawyers. They know how to look for that, and then they say, well, it's no good, it's a gray area. And they make it sound like it's bad, but they made it, they should have been smart enough to cover that. And so we have Cheyennes trying to do that. They are trying to use the gray areas over here, and it doesn't work.

CHAPTER 12

"This Is One Story That Needs to Be Told"

May 2, 2003

Because part of the Sacred Mountain, Bear Butte, is privately owned, the threat of commercial development is very real. The Arrow Keeper has long fought to protect it, along with other traditional Cheyennes and their supporters. On the day this narrative was recorded, Bill had just read some papers related to the fight.

SMS: *So you got those papers, and then you were sitting out here thinking.*

BRH: Well, you know, a lot of these things, I don't know what to do. So I'll go in the Tipi and then I'll start asking, well, then, if I'm supposed to be the Arrow Keeper and these Arrows come from there, should I go there and be represented or represent myself? And how come I can't go over there and say anything about all of this? Am I supposed to be there, or am I not supposed to be there?[1]

1. The Arrow Tipi, through Mahoz, is a place of instruction, where the Arrow Keeper seeks answers to troubling questions.

Is that the answer, that I'm supposed to be here? What's supposed to tell me? What's supposed to tell those guys to leave that alone, that belongs to Cheyennes, stay away from there? All of these things, I'm asking these questions. And then finally I come out and get tired, and get through praying. I mean, sometimes I do, I get tired of praying; so I come out and just sit down out here, and then I start thinking about other things. And then all at once Nellie comes over here, and Lauren [his granddaughter], and they sit down, and then I'm looking at how much joy this little girl brings to our lives. And we didn't have anything to do with it, but then we did; we do have something to do with it. But yet, because we're human, that's why we had something to do with it. But this other part, it's supernatural-like, it's above everything. So how could that be with this one? The real story is that the birth canal that they came through, this little girl came through, is almost like the birth canal of the cave when the Arrows come out. Then they bring joy and happiness to our lives. And without that, then it becomes something else, and they tear it down. It's kind of like genocide or something like that if they tear that down.

It would have to be something that's meaningful to people, as a woman giving birth to a child. And that was the way I understood it—that these Arrows were born. They came through this birth canal, and they came through this cave, and Sweet Medicine brought them to us. And then they bring all of this happiness to us. At the same time there is a lot of sorrow, even with this little girl, that's going to be. But right now, for now, we are just enjoying everything. So this is one story that needs to be told—that it's ongoing—this child's still here. This child's here, she's bringing happiness. It's the same thing. And this thing has to be bigger—by the mountain being how big it is, and by Maheo being who he is. It has to be that way. But these Arrows are still born. They come through the birth canal the same way as the baby comes through the birth canal. And after that, I felt real good about that. Then I thought, well, maybe I'll just write that and send that up there.

It's related to my grandchild. It's something real that still exists today. It started a long time ago, but it has to be Maheo's way of telling us a story that's so supernatural but it has to be understood in this way for us. That's what I think about it.

CHAPTER 13

"Everything Becomes Real When You Pray That Way"

May 2, 2003

SMS: *You're trying to introduce what makes it difficult to tell a story.*

BRH: The way I'm supposed to tell you, the way it's supposed to go, the way I'm being told that I'm telling it, and then when somebody differs with that, then they can understand why I'm saying it this way. That's what it's supposed to be.

If a wolf or an animal will chew his leg off to get away, and when this thing is happening, this birth of this baby is happening, when they eat the placenta and everything, I'm pretty sure they just bit the cord off. And it doesn't look good for them today, but it was necessary at that time. Because if you didn't have something to cut the cord, you still had to cut the cord; or if you weren't strong enough to pinch it off, then you had to do something like that. And that's the raw, natural way of doing things. So if an animal can do that, it's not farfetched for me to understand it, but it's in a different context; it's not the way of just eating a placenta like most animals do. But to them it's vitamins, it's what they need. It does

a whole bunch of things. Like when you had your baby and
she [Nellie] had her baby, there were a lot of things that were
taken away from you. I'm not saying that you guys eat that
thing [laugh], but you know, in the animal world, where we
learn these things from these animals, understanding it this
way to where at that time it was necessary. People do the
things they have to do. It's the same thing here, but it's in a
different context, and it makes it sound all right. But this is
the same thing; it's just in a different context. And somebody
else maybe wanted to try to elaborate on it and made it into
this other thing.

It was like the *Seven Arrows* book.[1] When it came out, a lot
of these guys were really upset with that. But the guy that

1. Bill's grandfather had this to say about *Seven Arrows*:
It came out in 1976. It's supposed to be about Cheyennes, but it's not.
From what I was told, what is written up in there, about our way of life and
our ceremonies, it is wrong, it has nothing to do with us. It's some kind of a
story, and we want our name taken out of it. We want people to know this,
we want this book stopped. We invited them to come to the Arrow Tipi,
Harper and Row and those Northerners, but they didn't come. Instead, they
held a big meeting up in Lame Deer, Montana, July 1974. They wanted me
to come, but I didn't go, I was afraid, they might trick me. We sent three men
up there to observe, they were not allowed to make any decisions. But these
Northerners, Joe Little Coyote, made some kind of agreement with Harper
and Row, after that meeting they wrote, this book was accepted by both,
Southern and Northern Cheyennes, but this is not true. these Northerners
came down here and offered 9,000 dollars to me, they wanted me to sign
some kind of paper, I turned them down. I don't want that money. In January 1977, we asked the Native American Rights Fund to sue Harper and
Row, but time had run out. (Schukies, *Red Hat* 128)
    And Vizenor says,
    [Charles] Larson reviewed *Seven Arrows* by Hyemeyohsts Storm as a
historical revisionist novel because it depicted survival and "aggressive
confrontations" between tribal people and the dominant culture. He
insisted that the issue of how representative a tribal author might be "to
his people" is a question "best left to cultural anthropologists." Storm was
denounced by some tribal elders for his personal interpretations of cul-

wrote that came down here, and he only lived on a reservation for so long, and then he went to the white world. That's where my perception is, that's why I'm here, is to try to do these things right.

[I ask him about the audiotapes of his grandfather made in 1978 by Stephan Dömpke. He mentioned the tapes during an earlier visit, and I have brought them up again. He asks Nellie to look for the tapes.]

BRH: The stories that are in there are about how our lives changed when the white man came. We are having to deal with it, and we're having to live the Cheyenne way, and then we're having to live when we go out there. And he's telling people that these things are happening, but you can make it through these things if you just try to understand what Sweet Medicine said. He's [Edward] explaining what Sweet Medicine laid out for the people. He said this one night in the house. And he was talking into this microphone the way he explains it . . .

SMS: Just like you are right now . . .

BRH: Yeah—well, it's mostly telling about why some of these things are happening, and the things that are bothering our people today. He's also telling us some of the things we are not supposed to do.

[Nellie brings the tapes and a tape recorder to the table. Bill turns on one of the tapes, and we hear his grandfather speaking in Cheyenne. Bill stops the tape and translates his grandfather's voice.]

---

tural traditions and for his pose as a member of the Northern Cheyenne. The paperbound edition of the novel was released over the objections of traditional tribal elders on the reservation. Such serious tribal matters are not the mission of anthropologists. (*Manifest Manners* 82)

BRH: He's saying it's good to talk about these things so that they can go on. So he's telling Maheo that he's getting ready to pray to him and that he's going to tell about some things, and that he wants Maheo to know what he's going to say. So he's telling him that he's going to speak about these things. He's saying that Maheo, you know a lot of things have come on us that are going to really make us feel bad, feel sad, that it has come this way, meaning the white people. It makes us sad, and it makes us not do good about these things, and that is what we are experiencing now. He's saying, "Maheo, I'm asking you, is there something that can happen?" That we don't want to keep feeling sad, feeling this bad way that we're experiencing.

I attribute it to everything right now, what's going on. From the tribal government to all the people that are fighting among each other. Like I was telling you, there are some problems out there, like in some of these families. The parents pass away, and some of the kids get the mother and father to give them all of the land without contacting these other kids. Well, see, they go and make a document. They take their father or their mother or their relative who has a lot of land, and they get a document that this old person, because they are taken care of, they feel humble at that time. And so the government turns around and says, okay, you want to give it to her. Well, it's all good the way they see it, but it's no good because they didn't call the other people over here that are a part of that. But then there's a document that the governmental official and these guys all signed and everybody looks at and says, this is the way it is, and then these people have to fight. Because the government should have turned around and said, "How many kids are there in this group that are alive today?" This should be one of the first things they say: "How many family members are on this land?" But they don't do that. And sometimes they do ask, but these guys already know how to manipulate things, use the gray areas, the loopholes, to get something done. It's hard to go against the documents, and then the people start fighting among themselves. We don't want to feel bad about these things—we want them to go right. But a lot of people know how to manipulate like the white men. They know how to cheat, how to steal money. They know how to do everything, but that's what the white man wants them to learn, because he wants them to be like him. And if he's got goodness, why, that's what they're thinking they're going to be, but it's not all about that; it's all about the whole thing that he's teaching. It's about land. It's about this way the white man doesn't listen to our oral history. And that's the main thing of everything—our oral history. It's all messed up. And then he's wondering why these tribes are fighting. Because he wants them to live the way he lives. They are causing more trouble among themselves because of the way they are signing these papers. Then he says this is a good way. We have a capitalist way. We want you to follow it. It's honest; it's just. It's not honest. It's not just. This is what he's telling everyone else. Then if you don't conform to that, you are a radical, you're a terrorist, you're a rebel. And then you have to fight for yourself because he's labeled you that. Just like in the McCarthy era—that's what they were doing. They were calling these people communists. So that's the whole thing behind all of this.

[Bill lets the tape run again, and we hear more of Edward's voice.]

He's really saying the same thing again. He's saying there's still more things that are making our people sick, our people not feel good about things. And he's asking Maheo for help in straightening it out. That's what he's asking. There is a lot that has come on us, and we're not feeling good about things.

Like our ancestry. There are a whole bunch of us yet who still believe, and we're trying to hang on to these things, and

that makes us feel good. But there are a lot of us who are lost
and don't follow this way. But that goes back; it's just another
form, how the government wants us to be in the melting pot
and good little taxpayers. So that's what a lot of those Indians are doing. They're going along with what the white man
wants, and that's what is causing all of the problems. But
there are a lot of us that are still following this way, and we're
still hanging on to what we have.

[The tape runs again. Bill speaks over his grandfather's
voice.]

We're still living. We still have our truth. The pipe is still
inside the Arrow Tipi. When you use the pipe and pray and
tell the truth, everything becomes real when you pray that
way.

[Bill turns off the tape. He repeats some Cheyenne words
from it.]

Somehow we need to try to understand; all of us need to
try to understand how these things go, about the truth. I
mean, that's what he's asking for. We still have the Tipi and
we still have the pipe. It's about truth. The people need to
know to come and pray that way. But a lot of them, when
they come, they can't humble themselves. And that's the way
we do. We humble ourselves for this Tipi, and they don't do
that. So you can't come that way. You have to humble yourself. I always try to explain to them I'm only here doing this
formality part, loading the pipe and everything. You're talking to them. You're pleading to them. And some of them
catch it, they understand it.

When I hear my grandpa's voice talking about these
things, I know it's been going on for a long time. I get down
because my grandpa's talking about it, and to me he was a
great man, and he's having a hard time. But at the same time,
through him, we got the [soldier] societies back together.
Now it's a little more organized than what it used to be but

it's not—I don't know if it will ever be one hundred percent. Well, it also makes me feel better, because then what I'm experiencing, it's no different. When you think about the pipe and the Tipi, and it's the only place you can go and the only place you can get help, it's the only thing I can do.

CHAPTER 14

"You Have to Go Way Deep"
May 3, 2003

Around 1981 or the early part of 1982, my grandfather made a vow to go through the Arrow Ceremony, and he was the Arrow Keeper. The vow was for the people. He wanted to pledge the Arrow Ceremony one more time. It's for the people. It cleanses them. Then I think around February he got sick. He had a heart attack. He was by the Tipi. He fell, and when we took him to the hospital, they couldn't revive him. Six o'clock the next morning, he passed away. Then it became hard. [Long pause] I got upset with the Tipi and everything and said some things. But I later on decided, I figured out that I can't go that way, I can't continue that way. So it was just kind of making peace with the Arrow Tipi, and my grandfather had gone.

When he died, it was like my guts were wide open. I was vulnerable to any attack, and so that made me go deep into my prayers. I kept doing that, and I went to the chiefs and asked them if they would let me go through it [the Arrow Ceremony], and they said yes, it could be done. It was my grandfather's vow. And so that year went by and they didn't do anything about it, and I went back to them again. Then I went back to them again the next year. So they didn't want me to go through. Anyway, later in the story you will find out that that was part of the process of why I'm the Arrow Keeper also. I was scared. I thought I might not live because I didn't go through with the vow for four years. It's considered that way in Cheyenne law. So the last time I went over there, my grandma talked to me. And my dad took me over there, and he said you have to go in there and ask your grandpa, Joe Antelope. [Joe Antelope was Arrow Keeper at this time.] So we got there early in the morning. We waited there by the Tipi. My grandmother had told me that when you go there to ask your Grandpa Joe, she said, "He's my last blood relation, and if he turns you down, I don't want you to get mad at him. I want you to come back here and tell me, and then I'll tell you what you need to do." Well, I asked him if he would take me through, and he was scared to say yes or no. And I guess these other men, they didn't want me to go through because they knew that if I went through the Arrow Ceremony at that time, then I would be Arrow Keeper at that time. Because that's the way it goes, and the traditional law of it works that way. So I let my grandpa off the hook by telling him that, well, "Grandpa, Grandma said to tell you that if you turned me down, that I'm not to get mad at you or say anything bad to you." And then he looks at me and says, "Well, no, Grandson." So then we came out, we cried together, and when I got back home, I went to my grandma, and then she said she would tell me what to do.

So I guess my grandma called your dad, and she asked him. She said I needed to go to Bear Butte, and the whole family needed to go, and that she wanted to go. And the way that I understand it, Karl went to the dean or somebody, and the guy told him that this is your whole allocation for this year, so when you get in the van, and you get this money, don't come back and ask me for any more money for the rest of the school year [laugh]. So what he was actually doing was really sacrificing also. So everybody was sacrificing, I guess. So he came down, and we got in that big ol' Dodge van and we took off to Bear Butte. We went a different way. We went to Bear Tipi on the way to Bear Butte. Well, it's really important, too, that when your dad went and fasted, there were these men over there. George Elk Shoulder wanted to paint my grandpa. I think the argument was that he wanted to paint my grandpa, but the other men said, "No, he's the Arrow Keeper; you can't paint him," and so he painted your dad. And the thing is that they were talking about that, and so one day I asked them, I said, "Why doesn't anybody ever fast by Sweet Medicine's cave?" They said, "No, no; they might run you down from there, and then what are you going to do?" But if anybody did, it would take a strong person to do that. Well, when we left here, I didn't tell him [Karl] about it. I was fighting myself as we were driving up that way. I was thinking, no, you can't do it, because if you get run down, then what do you have? There's no way to save face. So anyway, we got up to Bear Tipi, and we started going along a trail, and we stopped off to the west and went down some rocks. [Those present were Bill, his grandmother Minnie, Nellie, all eight of their children, and Karl Schlesier.] Grandma started telling this story about Bear Tipi—she started telling the story about Bear Tipi. And everything that she was telling the story about, it was all there. The hollow tree story, it was a kid game. It was a kid game that they would run and hide, and some would go into this place. And then this guy would have a stick, and he would split the tips and put it in there and he would—this is how you get rabbits out. You put it in there, and when it tangles in the hair, you pull them out. So they used to do that, and some of the kids would have different kinds of hair, and then they would put it on a stick so when it was pulled out, it was a skunk or some kind of animal. It was a game. So when they got to where it was bear hair, it was "bear lady" [chuckle], "bear woman."

So when they said that, "bear lady," then everybody scattered, because then bear lady came out. But this story, somehow it was a real bear lady that came out. When it came out, it became larger. So this boy and this girl, they were brother and sister. And they ran, and the bear was after them. So they ran a long ways, and they came to some animal, and this animal was a mountain lion. And so the kids asked the mountain lion if the lion could fight her so that they could get away, and so the mountain lion said yes. But the bear killed him, so they went on to another animal—it was a big buffalo. And they asked the buffalo if he could stop this bear coming after us. So anyway, this thing, when it first started out, she turned into a bear, and she caught these two. In the big tipi they would feed her and kind of care for her. So the little boy would go out hunting and bring it home, and they would feed the bear lady. So one day the older sister figured out that they could shoot her in the foot with a bow and arrow, and then they could get away. So there was something that they used to have to rub on her feet because her feet were cracking, and so they did that. The girl raised the tipi cover up, and he shot her in the foot, and then they took off. This gave them time to get away. Then they come to the mountain lion, and then the buffalo, and then a big man. She defeated him. So they went on. It gave them a chance to get away—by this one fighting. And so they come to this rock on the ground. It was the only thing they saw. And so they asked this rock if the rock could save him. They said Cheyenne words, and then the rock said, "Well, I'll try my best." And these kids had to say some Cheyenne words, and then the rock grew big. And then she told them to close their eyes, "and then I'll tell you when to open them, and you tell me if she's this big." And so the rock grew and told them to open their eyes, and they looked and then they said, "No, she's still bigger than this." And then the rock told them to say some Cheyenne words again, and then they closed their eyes, and then the rock grew some more. And then the rock said, "Is she this big?" And on the fourth time, the kids thought the rock was big enough. And then in the meantime the bear lady was coming. So she gets there, and the rock is real big, and so she's trying to jump up onto this rock. And she scratched the rock trying to jump up there and scratched it as she was coming back down. So after a while she gave up. And that rock was really trying to help them, and so they were asking the rock if there was anything the rock could do that could defeat her. And so the rock opened up. Then when she went in, well, the rock closed on her. So as far as we know, she's there now. And then if you say these words, what she is, over there at that time, then she'll come out.

But anyway, in the meantime, these kids are up there, and they're starving; they can't get down. So people say a chief came along and saw them and told some men if they could make some different kinds of arrows with different feathers on them, whoever shoots the arrow that brings the kids down could marry his daughter. So men came from all over, bringing these arrows to try because these two kids are starving up there. And so eventually the first young man came up, and he shot one of the arrows up there. And the arrow turned into a bird and tried to grab them and tried to fly with them, but the bird wasn't strong enough. So they called out again for another man, and he came with a different set of arrows with different bird feathers. So they shoot the arrow up there, and the arrow turns into a bird and flies and tries to go and pick up the kids. And he can't do it—he can only lift them so high and lets them go, and then the bird flies off. And then the third man comes up. He has an eagle feather on the arrow, and he shoots it up there, and it changes into that bird and tries to fly to grab the kids, but they are still too heavy—the bird's not big enough. So then Sweet Medicine comes along, and when someone shoots his arrow up there and it turns into this golden eagle, then it was that arrow that got the kids off. And so then that man who shot up Sweet Medicine's arrow that turned into the golden eagle, he married the chief's daughter. It goes on and on from one story to another story. That's one about Bear Tipi.

Grandma told the story when we were there, and it seemed like everything that she spoke about was there: the rocks, the terrain, the trees, us sitting there in the grass, everything, and then the story was being told to us. We became the people that they were telling the story to. We became the future people—they told us the story.

Then we went on to Bear Butte, and I was still fighting with myself, whether I should go up there or whether I shouldn't. I don't want to say these words, because you can't just have these words. You can't just have these words. I mean, these people out there just can't have them. Everything that I learn I have to earn, so they have to earn it. So that's the only way you can get it. You can hear it and everything, you can speak it and everything, but it's not going to be so. So anyway, we went on to Bear Butte and we got there. And the morning I was going to go up, it was kind of cloudy like this, kind of rainy and cold. Didn't want to go [laugh]. Kept sitting there and talking, and, man, I don't know, and then I started talking with your dad about it, whether I should—whether I think I'm strong enough to go and fast at the cave. At the same time, I don't think I am, because I don't want to get run down. If I do get run down, you know, all hell breaks loose on my life. So anyway, finally I told Karl, "Okay, let's go." So we left. Bryan, Rondeau, your dad, they carried my stuff. The four of us went up there. Anyway, they left me up there, and I went to the cave site. And whatever's going to happen is going to happen. And so they leave, and then, well, I had to smoke my pipe four times and I had to sleep four times. And each time I smoke my pipe, I move to a different position and go to another place. And each time I saw four different things. One of them, there was a little green man, and he was sitting on some rocks over there, and he was shaking his legs; he was looking at me just watching. But when I went and got closer, it was just rocks and nothing else. The pipe closed up after that first one. It blocked up. That's probably part of the process I had to go through. It blocked up. I couldn't unplug it. But then I got the pipe again, and then there was something over here—there was a man in a tree looking at me. I could see his face. I was praying. I looked up and saw his face, and I thought, who is that? It started to scare me, too, you know. So eventually I turned around to look real good, and it was where a branch had broken, so the white inside, the pale-colored face like, that's what it was. But it looked like a real person looking at me, but that's what it was. So I finally went to another place. I left over there, and I went to another place that was on the side of a trail, a deer trail, and it was where the deer sleep. They make indentations on the trail and then kind of dig out a little bit like that [describing with his hands], and you can actually lay in there without falling off. So I laid there, and I was crying. And so I was praying, and this chickadee just kept making noise by my ear while I was praying this way. But it was—he came to take my prayer. So anyway, I laid down and covered up, and I was going to sleep again.

The last time I went to sleep, and I had my head covered, this buffalo came walking out. And I could feel his breath, you know—he was just breathing. I was right in the trail, and I just remember these trees going down, and I thought the only thing I could do was just throw the cover off and just dive, go down the hill. I mean, it was almost straight down. So I figured if I could just grab a tree and go this way, then the buffalo will go on. Hopefully [laugh]. That's a lot of calculating [laugh]. But anyway, I finally get my nerve up, and one, two, three, and I'm going to go. And I throw the thing over and I start to jump, and looked—and there was no buffalo. So it was just something like, it happened but it didn't happen. It was just something that had to happen like that, and then it had to show me that it wasn't real. Oh, and there was a little pond up there. There were weeds growing around the pond—square weeds; they weren't round. I brought some of them down. Well, after that, then, I don't know, it was late afternoon and I came on down. Anyway, as I was coming down, there was this guy, this Northern Cheyenne with the glassy, smoky eyes, the white eyes [a sun gazer].[1] Joe Fox and I were walking down, and he came out of his tent. And I guess he didn't see me, and then all at once I came up on him and he turned around, and man [laugh], his cloudy eyes—gray, almost white, though you could tell there were eyes on the bottom. But the white was more pronounced until you looked good. So I looked at him and he asked me, "Who are you?" And I told him who I was and who my grandpa was, and he asked, "What did you do?" And I told him I fasted. He asked, "Are you through?" I said, "Yeah, I'm through now." He said, "Where did you fast?" I said, "On the north side where the cave is." Man, his eyes went big like that, and he looked at me for a long time and said it was good. And so we went down.

That trip was to come back, coming back, because I had to stay away from the Arrow Ceremony for four ceremonies. And it was what I already knew in the beginning, when these Cheyenne men came to get the Arrows the day after my grandpa died. And we went in the Tipi, and there I told the men right there that, you know, I can stop you guys from taking these Arrows, but my grandfather said if they come ask for them to let them go. So that's what I'm going to do. And I said we're going to cry because they had been here a long time. But some of these men knew that if I went through my

1. Sun gazing is a ceremonial procedure in which an individual looks directly into the sun for an extended period of time in an attempt to make contact with the sun spirit, Atouz.

grandfather's vow, that there would be nothing they could do. They would have to give me the Arrows. But then I think these mistakes have to happen. Because after that, after they went and took the Arrows, a lot of things happened during that time, 1983, the next year.

I'll tell you about Dan Rather where he made that statement on TV. See, my grandfather used to watch Walter Cronkite every evening. After he would get through eating, he would go turn the TV on and sit and watch Walter Cronkite. So I guess it was my turn. So I was watching Dan Rather, and Dan Rather said that since 1955 the United States had tried to shoot a ballistic missile off a Polaris sub to hit a target in Nevada. And since 1955, they have all landed in the sea. So they would land in the sea. So Dan Rather said, "Today"—it was in 1983—"they made their first successful launch." So by praying and asking about these things, what actually happened was that, like, the Arrows were up like this [motioning], and so no rockets could come in because of that, because of my grandpa and these other Arrow Keepers before him. So they were always up. So when the men made a mistake by taking them to Joe, what they thought they were doing was a great service, but they actually pulled the Arrows down. So that was the first successful launch after he passed away.

And from that time on, I'm pretty sure I got them back up. It was something that had to happen. If you're on the road to learning something, you have to lose something that's very, very dear and important to you. But then you have to take that and understand it as that and don't lose it in vain. You have to learn from that. You're not going to know anything, but you just have to keep praying and praying. You have to keep asking and asking. You have to, and then what happens is really something. I mean, it's really something to be proud that Grandpa had to show me this way. So instead of being real sad all the time, I mean, there's time for mourning, but if you really want something, you have to learn something.

You learn something. That's the only time. That's when the alcoholic finally goes to the lowest low, that's when he starts coming back up, but not until then, not until he's gone his deepest. It's the same way in life: you have to go low, you have to go way deep, and the deeper you go and the harder you are truly trying to understand it, the better off you are going to be. But if you just feel sorry for yourself all the rest of the time, then you know nothing. Then you're not really feeling sorry that you lost somebody; you're feeling sorry for yourself. So that's part of it. It's something real hard. That's part of what I know.

I have many dreams, and many things come to me, real, I mean, real, real, and I can prove it to myself the next day that they were real.

CHAPTER 15

"That's How You Get There"

May 3, 2003

SMS: Yesterday you were talking about how certain people don't respect oral history. You're very conscious of language and how it can be used against a person. I'm thinking about how language works.

BRH: The contrary was someone that was invincible because he did things backwards.[1] So when you say something both ways, there's nothing they can use to get at you. You have to

---

1. Among the Cheyennes, there were two types of Hohnuhka, or contraries. One consisted of men who carried a Hohnuhkawo, a Thunder Bow, which is a spirit lance in contrary form—in other words, a lance in the form of a double-curved bow. The second type of contrary was organized in the Hohnuhka Society. These contraries were medicine people, both men and women, who had a special ritual and served as healers and hunters in the Massaum Ceremony. For further discussion of the Cheyenne contrary, see Dorsey, *The Cheyenne: I. Ceremonial Organization;* Hoebel, *The Cheyennes;* Grinnell, *The Cheyenne Indians;* and Schlesier, *The Wolves of Heaven.* The concept of the contrary is similar to the Apache and Pueblo clowns who act in opposition to the sacred. The Cheyenne contrary is also related to the trickster phenomenon that permeates many North American tribal cultures.

figure it out to say it. The contrary didn't do it every day. He did it in ceremonies. It's the way things are made; it's like the yin and the yang, how it goes around, black and white. They can't say anything against you because you've said it both ways. It closes it up and yields it safe.

SMS: *Can you give me an example of how you might use that idea when you deal with someone, or in a particular situation? I mean, I am trying to understand what that would mean.*

BRH: [After a considerable silence] So, like, someone comes to see me and he's mad at me. He comes to the door. Before I say, "Hello, how are you doing?" I say, "Have you come in a good way?" And if he says yes, then I have nothing to fear, because if he changes that himself, it goes back to him. I've defused the opposition. If he says, "No, I'm not feeling good about something," then I have to be ready; that puts me on my guard. Because he's coming in telling me the truth.

SMS: *Do you often think about that when you interact with people or when you deal with people?*

BRH: Yes. It's just like a man coming over here. He has to stop four times; he has to tell these guys—these guys are guardians of me, so they ask him, "What have you come to see the Arrow Keeper about?" And so he tells them, "I've come in a good way." And he goes a little farther, and they stop him and they ask him again, these headsmen; they ask him, "What have you come to see the Arrow Keeper about?" And so he tells him again. So on the fourth time, he's at the door. And then I wait until he says, "I come in a good way," and if he doesn't say that, it's on him. So these guys that were guarding me, they have cleared their slate; so they're not obligated to stop him because he has told them four times why he has come in a good way. So these guys will remove themselves, pull themselves out of the way, and let him come in. And if he's already made a mistake by not saying that, when he comes in, it's Maheo, it's not me.

SMS: Does that happen sometimes?

BRH: Yeah. Everybody is told, "This is a Tipi of truth. You have to only speak the truth." So right there we're off the hook by telling him that, and then if he doesn't come in here and tell the truth, then he's on the hook, because from that time on, Maheo is taking care of it; it's no longer in our hands. And this guy realizes that. See, we'll believe him, everything he's saying. We don't have to have a lie detector there. We'll believe everything he's saying to us; we don't have to discount it. So there are several situations in which we can do that. It's just like Custer.[2] I mean, he came in and smoked,

---

2. Colonel George A. Custer occupies a prominent place in Cheyenne memory. On November 27, 1868, with his command, the Seventh Cavalry, he attacked Black Kettle's camp of fifty lodges on the Washita River. With a loss of three officers and nineteen troops, Custer's force killed approximately fifty women and children, a handful of warriors, and Black Kettle. Custer quickly withdrew his force when Indian reinforcements rode up from camps farther down the river. Among the prisoners taken was Mo-nah-see-tah, the teenage daughter of Little Rock, a chief who had died protecting the fleeing noncombatants. In *Halfbreed: The Remarkable True Story of George Bent—Caught between the Worlds of the Indian and the White Man,* Halaas and Masich write that "By his own account, Custer found the slain chief's daughter vibrant and beautiful, and officers and scouts with the Seventh contended that the commanding officer not only took her into his care but into his bed as well. Cheyenne tradition corroborates this, holding that Mo-nah-see-tah bore Custer's child late in 1869" (261).

At the Battle of the Little Big Horn, Mo-nah-see-tah and Custer's son Yellow Bird were present in the Cheyenne camp when Custer's troops were annihilated, and she was close by when Cheyenne women took the wounded colonel's life on June 25, 1876. Cheyenne elders firmly believed

and they talked Cheyenne to him, and then he would probably go out and say, "Well, that's gibberish; it doesn't mean
anything to me." That's what he would probably tell his fel-
low soldiers, but . . . [laugh] So these things, there are several
switches that we use to turn these on. And this guy can come
in here, and he can defuse all of it by saying the truth. But if
he doesn't, then he has done this to himself. It's not the Tipi,
it's not the Arrow Keeper; we've told him all the way,
because he is asked during the whole process. So even
though he hates me or whatever, dislikes me, I still have to
protect him all the way, and I have to believe what he's saying. And the final part of that is that when he finally gets to
there, then he's actually asking Maheo.

It's really serious. I mean, some people look at this thing
[the Tipi] as a rag held up by so many poles. Some do look at
it that way, you know. It's right on the ground. The ground
is dirty. The ground is alive.

I always have to protect just about everybody. All I have to
do is just be good to everybody. It's knowing these things.
But it's learning these things. It's not learning that is like a
form, let's say, "Okay, first you approach this man with sage.
Next you ask him what you need from him. And okay, here
is where you cry" . . .

---

that his end was presaged by what had happened on March 15, 1869. With
the bulk of two cavalry regiments, the Seventh and the Nineteenth Kansas
Volunteers, he had been ordered once again to strike the Cheyennes. He
located the Dog Soldier camp in which stood the Arrow Tipi. When the
warriors rode out and formed a skirmish line, Custer refused to attack,
instead sending a message that he had come to make peace. He was led
into the Arrow Tipi, where the Arrow Keeper, Stone Forehead, smoked
with him before the Sacred Arrows. After the ceremony, Stone Forehead
emptied the ashes on Custer's boots, warning him that the Arrows would
kill him if he broke his promise. Various sources that discuss these events
include Berthrong, *The Southern Cheyennes;* Hyde, *Life of George Bent;*
Halaas and Masich, *Halfbreed;* and Miller, *Custer's Fall.*

SMS: *You're saying if someone really wants to know what's going on, they have to dig for it.*

BRH: They have to figure it out.

SMS: *That's ideally the way I see this thing. Let's say a Cheyenne reads this in a hundred years, and they find out who the Arrow Keeper is, and they go to that person and say, "Well, here's what the Arrow Keeper said in 2003." And then that's just one piece of the puzzle for that Cheyenne a hundred years from now to figure things out, based on what you've said, based on what your grandfather's said, and on and on. I mean, that's ideally the situation, not putting things down that shouldn't be put down.*

BRH: [to Nellie] Where's that Father Powell book? Can you get it? Just grab it right quick and let me show her what I'm talking about. [Nellie goes to look for the book, *Sweet Medicine* by Peter Powell.] Well, you probably know it. [Nellie stops looking.] In the book there are references to who said this stuff. Okay, now there's Southern Cheyennes in the book, but you're reading the whole book; it says something about Kiowas, and it's written into this Cheyenne book. If you want to really be thinking, understanding, if you go back to the back of the book and look for all of the Southern Cheyennes, what pages, and then if you go and read all of those parts, that's when you know. Because if you read the whole book, you're all cluttered up, you're all screwed up. All of these other people are in this book, and if you read it, it will be foreign to you. The only way you are going to do anything about Southern Cheyennes is to just go look for the Southern Cheyennes in the back.

But you have to think about it. You have to suffer; it's about learning where you're at. It wasn't easy for you. And you have to do it yourself. You couldn't have Sedna do it, or your dad do it, or your mom do it, and then finally go over there and get your certificate. It would have been worthless, I mean. So that's what I'm saying. Everything is so simple. It's right there in the leaves, in the trees, in the plants, in the ground. It's out there, but they're looking for some sophisticated line. A sophisticated line. For them, sophistication is up there. But they're not going to find it. You're going to hear some great quotes, but they're not going to find it. But to me it's just simple. It's thinking about it, praying about it, meditating on it, and eventually it comes to you. You don't see it; it's not a flashing sign or something—you never see it that way. It's just something that you just kind of flow into. It just comes to you. There's no set guidelines, well, like say a parenting book. There's really no parenting book. I mean, it's only telling about somebody's little things, things that happened to them, and that's all right in a way if you know how to look at it and use it for your benefit. And that's all I'm saying. They can find all of this. But all they need to do is look in the Father Powell book or any other book and read what is said about that person or what that person is saying. That's the way it is. But still you need to find it, you have to figure it out. But that's part of your lesson, that's part of your learning, and that's how you get there.

CHAPTER 16

"In Cheyenne Life It's All One"

September 20, 2003

The way I've taught my kids, they respect more their privacy. There is privacy inside this house. All the boys would go out if the girls wanted to take a bath, and if the boys wanted to take a bath, all the girls would go out. And it's respected so much. The respect that comes from that, from being close to the edge.

They are taught to respect each other's privacy. They learn to respect each other I think more than the average child. They have control of themselves to where that—it's like the way they say the fox guards the hens. Everybody knows that the fox is going to grab one of the hens, but in this environment it's not. I mean, they're put on the edge to where they understand it and that they respect that way, so they're more respectful in things than most people would be. And by putting them in a close environment like that, in the future it will be up to them if they want to go a different way. It's up to them; it's not up to me. If they want to go back to that way, they can. They will realize that in order to do that, you have to work and do all of these things to provide a shelter and everything. It's the same way here, but they're doing it, they're living it: they're living the door, they're the door, they're the curtain. They understand it more than most people would, and so by having them in a tight environment where you can still respect, then you won't end up like the fox reaching in and grabbing the hen. The way I taught them is that if I had a chance, I could teach the fox and the hen to live together, and that the fox would never bother the hen. But that's just my teaching.

[In the house we watched a video, *Winds of Change*, narrated by N. Scott Momaday. In the next passage, Bill is responding to this video.]

It's no good. It's a corrupt system. It goes against traditional people. See, we have two tribes here. The Navajo only have one tribe. We are having to coexist with the Arapahos, but we have two different ideals. In other words, you're putting, I guess, a Catholic and a Protestant in the same building. Now, how do you understand that part? [laugh] It's the same thing. It's got us in the same hole, and then we're going to try to get along to get out. This Catholic and this Protestant, they're going to stay in that hole [laugh].

The system is separation of church and state, so that's what they're trying to do here, but in Cheyenne life it's all one—religion and living and doing business, it's all one. And the other way is a separation of church and state.

SMS: What does it feel like to see the Cheyenne come together for the ceremonies?

BRH: The ceremonies rejuvenate the people. It's plain and simple. You go and do things right, and you pray and you feel good, you go on. At the ceremonies, I feel great when a lot of Cheyenne come together for the ceremonies, because I'm not worried about what the business committee is doing. It has nothing to do with what we're doing there. And they're saying that they respect it, but then they go out and do whatever they're going to do. Just like this year, they got some money, and they sent some old people to Bear Butte. And we're over here doing the ceremonies, and that means that nobody is supposed to cross from here to Bear Butte—and then you have these people crossing over there. So they sent some elders over there, and then they come back over here and want me to pray for the elders that might cross over there. Well, why did they send them up there in the first place during that time? They don't even care about what's going on. They were sending a bunch of people in front of the Arrows, and they could get hurt.

It's all these mistakes that they make. They send people to die. I mean, the space shuttle, you look at it right now, but how many people died to get that up there? They're not doing things right. Now they have pictures of it all falling down. But their success is motivated in that, well, we know we're going to have collateral damage. We know we're going to lose some people. But let's keep it to a minimum, and then we'll all hurray and have parties and everything. I mean, that's going on constantly. That's not just with the space shuttle; it's with every endeavor that they ever tried. So it's working. But somebody else dies in that process. So many people, just to get the safety belts on, I mean. So many people died before they ever did anything about that, but there's nobody saying anything about all of that. They have statistics and everything, but those are just numbers. You don't cry about numbers. It's not close enough unless it happened to one of yours. And you are the only ones crying, so it's not working. I mean, if people are willing to, if the Cheyennes are willing to go ahead and get their legs cut off [due to diabetes] and do all of that, then it's working. But if they want to be like veho and do all of the things he's doing, then don't come cry to the Tipi that you're losing your legs or you're going blind, you know.[1] But I can't tell them that [chuckle]. I can't tell them, I can't say that, but that's what they think. They come over here, they come to the Tipi, they want to get well.

---

1. "Veho" is the Cheyenne term for "white man." It means "spider."

CHAPTER 17

"These Things Have a Power"

September 20, 2003

Before I began taping our conversation, Bill showed my sister and me a sign that had been made and put up at the ceremonial grounds. He said that it had taken a while for him to figure out what it should say. Since outsiders were trying to cause some difficulties, Bill thought that it was extremely important to have the proper wording on the sign. For example, they wanted the sign to say that firearms were not allowed on the grounds, but because guns are sometimes given as gifts as part of the ceremonies, he was afraid that if the sign said "No firearms," the police could come in and accuse them of violating their own laws. They finally came up with the phrase "No unauthorized firearms."

BRH: The first day we moved in, we had thought about the sign, but we couldn't come up with the words. And so we went on ahead, and so we moved up there, and then the police showed up that evening after we had gotten the camps up and everything. So the police showed up, and a lady came driving by and stops by the Arrow shade, the Arrow Tipi, and says there are some cops—there are some cops down there, and they're checking people. And so I sent a chief and a headsman down there to go see. And so they went down there and talked to them, and the cop said to them that they had jurisdiction on certain parts of that land. And a headsman told him, "No, you don't." But the cop said he would bring the papers the next day. So the next evening he brought the paper to show where he had jurisdiction, and then there was a guy in a black FBI uniform. He was just sitting there not saying anything. Well, they brought the paper up to me, and then I had to figure out what we had to do. So I went and prayed. And the next morning a guy came to the shade, and I asked him, "Can you make a sign?" And he said, "Yeah, what do you want on it?" So I told him. He wanted some other things on there, but I told him, "No, it has to be said this way." So he went back, and then he had the sign there that evening. So we put the sign up on the third day, and then we didn't see the guy in the black suit anymore.

What they're trying to do is, they can't create any more Sand Creek Massacres. Well, I don't know about that [chuckle]; anyway, they're not supposed to, but now they're trying to law us to death. So they're trying to law us to death, and then it takes us away from what we're really supposed to be doing, because we're having to talk to lawyers and go this way and that way. We have to go do all of that; we have to do research, and it takes time away from us. But it's going to hurt them as much as it hurts us, because they're not realizing what they're really doing. But they don't listen until something happens. You can't tell them anything.

SMS: *But everything worked out?*

BRH: Yeah, everything kind of worked out all right. But we have to do research like that, that sign, and we have to figure it out. Like I say, we can hurt ourselves. If we would have said "No guns," like I said, and then we brought guns on, then they would have said, well, you made the law, and you disobeyed your own law. I mean, it was just a simple word, to stop the whole thing, but the thing is that I'm not really into words or anything like that. I'm into this over here, how I'm supposed to pray over here. It's living in both of these worlds. It drives some Indians crazy, and then they go in the hills and they go drink because they're tired of living that way. They say, "I can't win." They have all of the guns, they have all of the manpower, they have everything. I mean, I don't know why they're worried about us.

A good thing to look at is *Indiana Jones.* I mean, it's saying something, and I think that's what they're trying to do. It's like this *Lord of the Rings.* They want the ring, and they want to be able to harness everything. You know it's been going on for a long time. You know, in *Indiana Jones* they found the ark, and all they did was put it in a warehouse. And when they showed the warehouse, remember the big scene where there were just stacks of people's sacred objects from all over the world—just a big warehouse full.

What they're not seeing is that these things have a power. If this man knows his rules and regulations on what he was given, there's no way he can hurt people. If he doesn't know, then he can hurt people. And they've been given for these reasons, to learn these things. I mean, if somebody reads a Bible and it says "Thou shalt not kill," and if he lives by that, think how things would be, you know? And if you do kill, then this way has a way of what they call the law of averages, because you can only do that for so long, and then it comes back on you. What goes around comes around; it comes back on you. So no man can do that and get away with that. You can do that for so long, and that's it. It's happening to them already, and they're not even seeing it. But it's happening to them already now. They're finding out. But then there's going to be a new group of people come in. So in the next twenty years after these guys died, they're not going to see what they had to go through, and so they're going to create a whole new system again. And then we'll have to turn around and guard against that. See, it's always something else, and now it's sovereignty. Now who's got sovereignty? They're tearing sovereignty down quick. It's like that sign— it holds it off for a few years, or maybe a year, and then we'll have to figure out something else again.

CHAPTER 18

"Sometimes It's Just Too Heavy to Carry"

September 20, 2003

I received an e-mail for my father from one of his former students, Stephan Dömpke, who worked on the action anthropology project with the Southern Cheyennes. For the past ten years, he has been working with traditional leaders in Kyrgyzstan to implement a project for the revitalization of natural sacred places in that country. Dömpke and the president of the Tengir-Ordo Foundation, Dastan Sarygulov, were in the process of organizing a conference on "Tengrianity: The Worldview of the Altaic Peoples," by which he meant "all peoples of Central Asia who trace their origins to the Altai Mountains in the very center of Asia, mainly the Turkic peoples." Dömpke wrote: "The conference aims to gather threads of knowledge from various fields and countries—mostly from Siberia and Central Asia—in order to explore Tengrianity, and wishes to establish links with other spiritual cultures in the world. Mr. Sarygulov has asked me to help him invite spiritual elders and scientists who could be helpful in this most important endeavor." The e-mail asked for my father's participation in the conference and requested that he "find a Cheyenne or other tribal leader who may, through his knowledge and experience, be able to help the people here in their quest."

Bill and Stephan know each other, so after I told Bill about the e-mail and explained the purpose of the conference, he asked my sister to go get the globe in the house. When she brought it outside, he took a small whisk broom and carefully brushed all of the dust off it. Then he brought it to the table and asked me to show him where Kyrgyzstan was. He asked for a piece of paper, which he used to make connections from Bear Butte to other places throughout the world, including Mt. Sinai.

BRH: Maybe something's coming together, I don't know. It's something that I do in here, I mean, I see in there [the Arrow Tipi]. I don't know, you got me thinking, because I never knew about some of these other sacred places. See, there's something: when we pray, we're praying to the four directions. Now, that's the groups of people, that might have a connection.

SMS: What would you say to these people if you had a chance to speak to them?

BRH: I would ask them about similarities, about things in their culture. But it would take some time.

SMS: How would you introduce yourself to these people?

BRH: The only thing I know is that I'm born into this, from Stone Forehead that smoked with Custer, I mean. By the people, I've been given the right to talk to Maheo. Otherwise, I'm just a regular ol' Joe. I'd tell them, "Hang on to your beliefs. Somebody told you something, you have to believe that." I think that's what I've done here.

SMS: Do you think it's an external fight, a fight against external forces, or is it an internal fight?

BRH: It's both, but the inside is harder. But then I think about the inside, it's Maheo's way of saying you're taking a test today. That's what he does. On the other part [the external] you can say and do things, but on this other part [the internal] you have to be careful, because on this part you're also dealing with people—but you're dealing with people here that you know, so you have to be careful what you say. If you're not, you can take your whole self down by not being careful.

In these past ceremonies, I finally just told them. They came to me, and they said, "Do you want us to go talk to them? We'll go talk to them, the societies, chiefs, and headsmen." And I told them, I said, "No, just let it come to a head. Let them come over here, and we'll deal with it when they get here." But then it just kind of went away.

[He is referring to criticism directed at him by some Cheyennes. The historical written record shows that Arrow Keepers have often been criticized by members of the tribe.][1]

If something higher is putting you out there, and he wants you to do things right but he's giving you ample opportunity

---

1. One of the great tragedies to befall the Cheyennes was the loss of the Sacred Arrows to the Pawnees; historical sources vary with respect to the date (usually either 1830 or 1833). George Bent's narrative of this tragic event reveals that some of the Cheyenne warriors present defied the Arrow Keeper (George Bent's grandfather). The appropriate procedures were not followed, and the Sacred Arrows were captured by the Pawnees. The Cheyennes made new Arrows after this great loss, and several years later the Pawnees returned one of the Arrows; another was returned by the Brulé Sioux after they had captured a Pawnee village. Two of the new set of four Arrows were then left in a bundle in the Black Hills, from where they originally came to the Cheyennes through their prophet, Motseyoef. The various sources that discuss the loss of the Arrows include Hyde, *Life of George Bent*; Grinnell, *The Fighting Cheyennes* and "The Great Mysteries of the Cheyenne"; and Powell, *Sweet Medicine*.

to mess up, then there's no use worrying about that. There's no reasoning on the other part because he's giving you opportunity to do things right, but there's more opportunity to do things wrong that he's given you. And so then finally you can mess up thinking you're doing right. And so the best thing is just let it come on, and if I'm not the person I'm supposed to be, then let it happen. And so nothing happened.

A higher power is challenging you, is asking you, are you the right person? He's saying that. Did I go wrong? Did I pick somebody wrong? Now you're the one that's on the line. So then you have to understand all his rules, and it's about people, compassion, everything, all of that; it's all there, but he's given you ample opportunity to go wrong. So in one sense you can look at it that way, and you can try to figure through this. But in the end it's still going to be the same thing; just let it come on. And then that way you'll feel better about yourself. If you're not supposed to be there, then they take you out. I mean, it gets heavy after a while. You're trying to do something for somebody, but you already know these somebodies that are coming, they're not willing to do that for themselves. Then why are you here trying to explain that to them? And you kind of wonder about that. Well, okay, I have to figure it out. They either want to be well or they don't want to be well. But they're lying to the highest things that you know—by going to the Jiffy Trip, doing whatever they want to do, mistreating their bodies. Then there is no use for that to be there for them. Because they've been given ample opportunity on everything. It's up to each individual.

There's still a lot of hurt going on, and in some ways you feel responsible. But they have their own brain; they can do whatever they want to do. If they want to do good for themselves, then they can do it. But you're still worrying about them, because they still come up and smile at you and shake hands with you and tell you you're doing good. But they're not doing good themselves because they're not doing what they're supposed to be doing. So, I don't know, it just gets heavy. Sometimes it's just too heavy to carry. I have to try to help them. They're my people. And I feel bad about it.

If it's just coincidence that I'm Arrow Keeper, then I'm living a lie. But if it's something that's been set out a long time ago, I can see all of that. But I'm not the powerful person that you're wanting me to be. I don't have all of that superhuman strength. I don't have—I mean, sure, I can pick up coals and move them and everything and not get burned, but there are times when I do get burned. But it's because of my concentration that I get burned. But when I'm into it, you might say I don't get burned. Now, I lose a lot of hair on my fingers [chuckle]; I have no hair on my fingers. It's a hard road, and you do things, and things get better, and then you go along for a while. And then they're not getting better, and then you go down, way down, and you have to crawl back out. And then you have to refocus on what you're doing, and then everything gets all right, it's okay. And then at some time it starts getting hard again, and then better, but you think about: Am I not praying the way I'm supposed to be praying? Am I not concentrating? What's happening? But I think everybody is given something wrong to do, and either they do or they don't.

I don't lose faith. I get tired. I feel good because there's nobody coming right now. But they won't be coming until maybe October, November, because a lot of them came to the ceremonies. When things start dying, why, then that's when it really gets heavy. Because then the trees start dying. You see the trees start dying, and you're sitting out here, and then they start coming.

CHAPTER 19

"That's Where It's Hurting My People"

September 10, 2004

Well, about Stone Forehead, there's a Cheyenne. He does something, he's named, he's given a name, and then later on through life he does something, some kind of a deed, or he becomes something, and then he changes his name. And so now, even today, some men have two or three names, and some reluctantly don't want to change their name, like when I was in 'Nam. Well, I came back and they had a victory dance for me, and Grandpa asked me if I wanted to change my name, and that they were willing to do that. They had gifts of money, and they wanted to do that for me, but for me, for some reason, I didn't want to change my name. I wanted it to be the same. [My Cheyenne name] means One Little Elk. Anyway, that's the way—if you translate it, that's the way it comes out. Some people have their own version of Lone Elk, One Elk, but anyway, [the first part of it] means elk, [the second part] means one, and [the third part] means little, so it means One Little Elk.

All right, anyway—I wanted for my name to be the same, but there are a lot of other Cheyenne men that wanted to go ahead and change their names, and for some reason or another they went on ahead and did that. And what I'm saying is that Stone Forehead was his name, and then maybe after he became Arrow Keeper, then they changed his name again, because it was Who Walks With His Toes Turned Out. And I just wanted to clarify that, because we're, through my grandmother's line, these are relatives, our ancestors. And Who Walks With His Toes Turned Out is one of the principal chiefs that signed the 1851 treaty, and that the United States government agreed through talking, dialogue with the people. And the people came up and told that these four main men should be the ones to sign the treaty and to deal with the government. And that's the reason that I'm bringing that up, is that I'm glad I'm through that line. This is my great-great-great-grandpa. The government and all the surrounding tribes all agreed what they were going to do, and these treaties were going to be the law of the land. That's the way it's supposed to be. But in the process they've changed it, and they went after different Cheyennes and used different Cheyennes that weren't the principal chiefs, that weren't the four main chiefs, the four main headsmen of this, the Cheyenne nation. They went around and got different people that would go along with what they were wanting to do, and so that's why I'm bringing all of this up. And I've always known that this line, this hereditary line, is where the Arrow Keeper comes from, and my lineage is through that. These are my ancestors. And I'm even so proud to think that maybe if that's the way, if people have heard it and told it, that Sweet Medicine is my grandpa also. So I feel real good about things that I understand, that I know. So anyway, I'm just kind of happy with that. And now we have gotten information on microfilm that has been printed way back to verify all of these things that I'm talking about. So anyway, I'm just kind of glad about that, that this Arrow Keeper line has, is hereditary, and that this new form of government that they've taken, the IRA [Indian Reorganization Act], is not a traditional Cheyenne

way of doing things—it's the veho's way of doing things, it's
the vash-ta-veho, and it's not a part of the Cheyenne Arrows,
it's not a part of the Cheyenne way, the Cheyenne way of life.
So anyway, this is just part of what I want to talk about, that
no matter what anybody tries to do or say, this line will live
on because of the Arrows. And there are other things on other
people's minds that they want to do things, but if it's not in
the Cheyenne language, it can't; it's not supposed to happen
that way. Well, they've tried to take the Arrows from me.
They've tried to do a lot of things, and they were never successful, because that's not the way it's supposed to go. And if
that was the way it was supposed to go, then they would have
been successful. So by understanding all of this, and talking
Cheyenne and understanding Cheyenne, that is one of the
main things behind being an Arrow Keeper. Also, your wife
has to be Cheyenne; your kids are Cheyenne, and your wife
has to understand Cheyenne and speak Cheyenne. And so
that's part of the rules and regulations also. And there have
been some changes in the past, but that's not proper procedure; but it's been done, and even though it's done, it doesn't
make it right. So you have to look at the whole, understand
the Cheyenne language. If you don't understand the
Cheyenne language, you'll never understand, or you'll never
be able to rationalize what's going on. If you've grown up
with the American language, that's the only way you're going
to be going, that's the only way you're going to be rationaliz-
ing things. But that's not Cheyenne.

So anyway, there have been people using some of these
things, what has been done in the past, and they're telling
the people that that's law, but that's wrong. Because where
they say that when the men, when the societies whipped the
Arrow Keeper, they're saying that it's all right for them to do
that. But they're not going on with the rest of the story. And
telling them that when these Dog Soldiers and Kit Fox [two
of the seven Cheyenne soldier societies] went against the

Arrow Keeper, they lost the Arrows to the Pawnees, and that was their wrong decision that they made. Even though that process was done, that doesn't make it right. So in that whole event, the Cheyennes had to suffer. And there was another incident later on in the 1830s. They whipped the Arrow Keeper, the Bow Strings, and they went on down to fight the Kiowa, and only one returned. They died down there for wrongfully whipping the Arrow Keeper and thinking that they were doing right. So some of these things, what some people, some young men, are telling people is that it's all right to whip an Arrow Keeper. But you have to be right; the Arrow Keeper has to be wrong. And if the Arrow Keeper's right and you're wrong, the men suffer the consequences of this action. So people need to know about that, people need to understand that. Yeah, you can do something, but that might be wrong, and if you do wrong, why then you and whoever else you have with you will suffer the consequences. Because there's truth and consequences in everything. And it's that way. It's a natural law, and it's going to always be there. No judge in the world, no Supreme Court justice, can make any laws against natural law. And they'll be the first ones to tell you that; the judges will tell you that. They cannot disturb natural law.

So anyway, I mean, it's just that these things are—you have to understand them, you have to know them, and you have to believe in them. And if you don't know them and you don't understand them, if you don't believe them, then you're misleading the people, and the people are going to suffer because of that. And we've had incidences where some men went after some young men to ask them to come help, and all these young men knew was that their old people, their grandmas and grandpas, moms and dads, told them when these old men come after you to come help, you don't refuse. So they, some of the men that were misusing this law, got some of these boys to come and help, and all they told them was that you're going to move tipi poles. And then on the way there, they told them that hey, when we get there, if we have to fight [chuckle], you're going to have to fight. And one of these little boys answered back and said that, "Fight? Fight? [chuckle] I didn't come here to fight; I just came to move poles." But what I'm saying in that situation is that that little boy followed the rules and regulations; he didn't refuse the old people, he didn't refuse the old men. But the old men misused that law, and these young kids had to suffer because of that. Because later on, their mothers and aunts and uncles brought them over to the Tipi to be brushed off. But because of the wrongdoings that these other men had used and told these people, they had to suffer the consequences of what happened.

It's about telling the truth; then they might get back on track. I want them to know, to understand that what we do now, the way we understand, the Cheyenne Arrow Keeper speaks the truth. So whatever is spoken, wherever we're at by the Arrows, that these Arrows represent the truth, and if the truth is spoken, long life is given. If you don't speak the truth, long life is not given.

There are people saying, like this one old lady, she went and told some people that were coming to us all the time, this old lady told this one young girl, "Oh, the Arrow Keeper doesn't like us. He witches us." And they came back and they told me that. If the Arrow Keeper witches against his own people, is he really an Arrow Keeper? Can he really be in that position? Is that what it's about? Is that what it's about? Now, that's what she feels. But I think if I've done that, I think Sweet Medicine and Maheo, they wouldn't know how to take care of that. Maybe that's been done in the past—witch people, wish harm to people. See, my grandfather always said, "Don't do anything offensive with your medicine. If you do something with your medicine and if you throw this medicine at that person over there, Grandson, that guy might know how to catch it and throw it back." You gotta know how to catch it if he throws it back. If you don't know how to do that, don't do that at all. So the best thing is to put a protection around you. So right there I know that. But that doesn't mean that Cheyennes didn't do that. But you have to know how to catch it back.

SMS: What do you think the greatest problem is for the Cheyennes right now?

BRH: Not speaking Cheyenne, not understanding Cheyenne. That's the biggest problem.

SMS: How can it be brought back?

BRH: It has to be brought back by a group of people that want to turn around and go back to the old way and not concentrate on going to work and paying for their bills and this and that. But there's several ways we can do that. It's just going back on your own land and living on your own land where you don't have to pay rent, you know. You see my house, and you see it's not very good, but I mean, it accomplishes what it's supposed to do. So if I can sit here and think and decide on what I want to do, it's my determination on how much I have respect and love for the Arrows. That's all it is. And if I only can come see them once a week, then I don't have that respect, then I don't have that determination, then I don't have that gumption. And I think that's where it's hurting my people.

Like, for example, we got $118,000 from the government for education. Man, everyone was all happy; man, we were all happy—hey, the kids get $118,000. So the government knows how to do this, these business committee people. Okay, the government sends the money down. There's red tape in that money to where that, okay, you have to have a group, you have to have a director, you have to have a secretary, you have to have a treasurer, you have to have members. So by the time all of these people took their money, these kids only got $9,000. That's the government red tape; that's their part. That was the red tape. That's from the government that they had to do that. And so the government sends money down, but you have to have a degree, a high school education, you have to have this, you have to have that. If you have all of that, you don't have time to do Cheyenne things. So the government and that way of life is deteriorating the Cheyenne way of life. Because they're saying that, well, we'll give you money, but you have to have all of these things.

CHAPTER 20

"That's How We've Come to Be Where We're At"

September 11, 2004

The reason why I'm saying that, like my grandfather, he would say, "Grandson, I got some men coming today; I want you to be here." Well, hauling hay and doin' what I had to do because I have eight kids, seven kids, six kids, five kids, you have to try to get them fed any way. But then old man wants me there, so that's why I had to be self-employed. And so what he was really saying was, well, I thought, Grandpa, I've heard it already before. I always tell myself, Grandpa, I've heard this story already before. But the importance of the whole thing was that when they told the story over again, there was a little bit of difference, if you were listening. This is what is important: if you were listening, every time some-body says something, it sounds like if nobody's not listening it's the same old thing, same old thing, same old thing. You know, I've heard it before: the guy's not listening, okay, but when you're listening, then all of these other points that are important come out. And so that's just what I really want to express and explain. So by me sitting there and Grandpa and talking with these guys, I'm basically just getting coffee and donuts, you know, just sitting here listening to what they're talking about. But the important thing, too, is that they're talking Cheyenne. So all of these stories that they're saying, it's really helpful now.

This is the main thing I'm trying to say. In thinking of one thing that's one way, but there's a reason why this part goes in over here. Because it went in over here doesn't mean— what I don't want you to get mixed up in is that saying something: "Well you said it here," but I also said it back there. I want you to understand that and to catch that, because to me it's really telling the story. It's the notes. To me it's the notes.[1] Well, anyway . . .

Well, we had thought about this a long time ago. I had already talked to some chiefs. I wanted to fulfill these three positions. And these positions can only be fulfilled by an Arrow Priest Chief. He has to make his chiefdom-ship first, and then he makes the Arrow vow, and then he is qualified to fulfill these three positions. Okay, so I started talking to older people—sixty, seventy, eighty years old. And I can't just tell them, "You have to make a vow." Because I can't mess it up, like just intimidating them and making them do something that I'm only thinking of, because then it'll appear that way to the other group, and the other groups. So by trying to tell them and explain to them, one has caught on, and the other one has finally decided later on that they—in the place and proper time that when they need to make a vow, they're going to make their vow, but not now. Okay, so then I got sick and I went into the hospital. And I didn't realize, or I didn't hear, that one of these men, Bryan's grandpa, nominated him to be in the chief's tipi, to be a chief. He didn't tell us until after-

---

1. This refers to an unrecorded conversation we had the previous day, in which Bill was talking about some of the books that people had written about the Cheyennes. To paraphrase his basic point, Bill said, "I wish I had all of the notes about what people had written about the Cheyennes—that would really give a lot of information, more information than the book."

wards, later on. Okay, this was a little after I got sick when I realized what went on between these guys in the tipi over there. They hadn't told me that. Nellie had said something, but I just didn't—it wasn't time for me to think about it serious. She had said something: "Hey, these men have asked your son something." But she didn't quite elaborate on it, either; but yet I knew that's what she was talking about. Okay, well, then, when Bryan—well, see, we had talked about this eleven-year situation, where my grandfather was the Arrow Keeper for eleven years and then he passed away, and then my father was only Arrow Keeper for three years. But he had passed away eleven years later. And then I became Arrow Keeper. And so I got my kids and sat down and said, "You know, you guys are going to have to think about things, on doing things on your own," without trying to tell them something. And so I was kind of getting worried, and I was kind of getting scared, because if that's eleven years there and eleven years there and then eleven years here, then that's also possible for me. So anyway, I went on ahead and tried to explain to them, every one of them, that you know people die and the world doesn't stop, and you have to go on. I mean, you'll be pissed, you'll be angry, you'll be, you know, and then eventually you'll accept the situation. But I mean, all of these things come in first. So I was getting them prepared. So then when I got sick, well [chuckle], that's getting pretty close. And then he called and he said he made a vow, a vow for me. And so then I didn't really realize anything at that time, because of being sick. It finally came into place later on. But kind of understanding some things, not really knowing, but it still wasn't quite clear. But anyway, then he made the vow. And then I went in, and I came out and I felt a hundred percent better. You can even see it in the photograph. I felt good, I felt great. And I even look skinny [laugh]. But anyway, that all started falling into place. But I'm still kind of worried, because Bryan still has to go through this thing. And then so we started

calling around and talking to people, and people started helping. And well, it was kind of difficult, but at the same time
everything was kind of going rough but smooth. It wasn't
quite smooth, but it was going. And then all of this other stuff
started coming in, surfacing: 1851, my grandpa's the one that
signed this treaty, all of these things. And then the four principal chiefs. So that's my position. And then when Bryan finished, when Bryan went through the Arrow Ceremony, I had
already started preparing. And so the next day, Monday, was
the chief's day. And so it was still doubtful, because then I said,
"Well, do I call all the chiefs or what?" Even if I did call them,
they're not going to be here until eleven or ten o'clock, because
they're nighttime chiefs and they don't do things early. And I
don't know why this chiefdom thing is going that way; they're
doing it in the dark when they're supposed to be doing it at six
o'clock in the morning, starting everything, and then by two,
three o'clock, they finish. I mean, I've seen it, I've seen them do
that. I've been there long enough to know that. That's the way
it used to be; that's the way it's supposed to be. Anyway, these
things all started falling into place, but not quite. So about six
o'clock that morning we woke up, and we got things ready
the way we're supposed to do. And then I was apprehensive
about what needs to be done. But I knew what had to be done
and how it had to be done and what we had to do, and it just
so happened that these certain chiefs are always in the camp.
So all I did was call them. I had the crier call them, and they
came. So that got done, and then I told my son, I said, "Well, I
think we're supposed to do this this morning." We wait until
seven or eight o'clock. When we do Cheyenne things in the
morning, in the daytime that represent with the Arrows, then
we need to do it now. So all of this all started falling into place
right there.

So Bryan had fulfilled his vow. So now the next thing was
to do what the Arrow Keeper does to place his son. So that
goes back from Stone Forehead to Black Hairy Dog; they

didn't get it done. So when they don't get it done, they allow—by them not doing what they're supposed to be doing, it allows the other men to pick, but if the Arrow Keeper gets all of his stuff done, then these guys can't pick; it's already been done. So then we just went through the procedures of placing him as Arrow Priest Chief. Okay, he's filled that position by doing what's supposed to happen naturally, and so anyway, we get that placed.

So the other chiefs, when they finally come, at ten o'clock at night, they're mad. They had even tried to call them to eat that day, but they didn't come until that evening. I'm sorry, but if they're not in camp, it's not our responsibility to go out and get them and bring them in. So anyway, they were mad that they weren't there. The problem is that they want to stay in the motel, they want to stay up there, they want to stay where it's cool, and they just now want to come in when it's dark.

It's the determination as to how you're going to get there, how you're going to set up things to be there. So I decided to haul hay, and that's not a good job. Who wants to lift all of those bales of hay? You know, hard work. Well, I had to choose that because nobody didn't want to do that, but then that's how I was going to get some money. But then I could pay people to go and do something for me, and so therefore I'm there in my grandpa's meetings. Because I've had to do a lot of hard work in order to do what my grandpa wanted. So they have to do the same thing. So if they want to stay in a motel and not be there when the sun comes up, you know, that's not my fault. I don't have any responsibility for that. I have to get up, I have to do these things early in the morning. And it's because of the job that's there that I put my foot in there. And so all of this is all falling into place because of the way things are supposed to be.

And so anyway, what we're doing is keeping things in order, and it's a big responsibility. But these things are followed by Cheyenne language. They're not just done because somebody thinks it should be right. And in the Cheyenne way there's no try—try to do this, try to get this done. There's no try. There's no such word in that instance. It's either you do it or you don't. So remember, I always tell you about my grandpa, he'd say, "Grandson, you got to. You just got to." That's what that means. It doesn't mean try. You have to do it. Those were the strongest words. It's the highest form of talking the way he understands it. So he's always told me that: "You got to." So there's no try; you either do it or you don't. So we've done it. And anyway, it all comes down that all these things fell into place. They were done for a reason. They weren't just done just to be right, just making a vow, just to be making a vow. Because if you make a vow, it's with Maheo, it's with Sweet Medicine, Motseyoef. And that carries a lot of weight, in that when I went through, when I made a vow, and with all the things that I had to go through, came the ability. And the understanding is when other men that didn't make a vow that tried to go after the Arrows, they all bounced back, whereas when I went after the Arrows, I didn't bounce back; we got the Arrows. But it was because somebody was doing something wrong. It wasn't because we thought it should be done that way; it was because somebody had done wrong. And by knowing these things and understanding these things, that's how we've come to be where we're at.

CHAPTER 21

"These Things Were Given by Maheo"

September 11, 2004

Well, to me, Sweet Medicine, I don't know how he was. There's stories as to how he was, but we don't know if that's the truth or not. But that's what we go by. We go by that; everybody goes by what he's heard. But if you ask me, he had to be somebody that Maheo was willing to give him something. He had to be. Some say he killed a chief; some say he did this and did that. Well, to me, when Maheo does something and takes somebody, that's so high a place to be put into by him. And he was allowed to go to Bear Butte, Nowahwus, and he fasted there. And then the story goes he was given these four Sacred Arrows. But there are other stories that he was given some things. I just remember a few stories. One of them was a bundle, and when he opened the bundle, the enemy just fell dead. Sweet Medicine turned around and gave it back and said, "This is too powerful." So Maheo probably gave him that chance to make that choice. And maybe Maheo was telling him that if you take this one, then you're not the right person. So he went back and gave that back and said, "That's too powerful." And the other was that it would heal the dead. Anyway, eventually it was the four Sacred Arrows, because they were powerful enough to take care of the people, but they weren't powerful in a bad way to kill everybody. They were given so that when they were pointed at the enemy, the enemy was confused. But then it's saying that they were given these things by Maheo through this Sacred Mountain to be given to them to use for their protection throughout life, or time. And so from whenever that was, they were given these things. And so throughout history, they traveled with us. And at certain times, it wasn't that the Arrow Ceremony was held every year. It was only when the people had problems. So it might go ten years, or longer, before they even had an Arrow Ceremony. So these things were given by Maheo. That's somebody else higher than anybody else that we understand. Compared to God, maybe that's him; it's just the Cheyenne language for him. I don't know; we just have the Cheyenne language for him. I don't know, but that's as far as what we know. Maheo, the creator of everything, who has made everything. For Sweet Medicine to get these things, he has to do right. And so Sweet Medicine, as far as we understand, he did right. And that's part of our ceremony, and we still honor that, and we still do that. If you don't do things right, I think things can happen. And that's what scares me: whenever I do something, I have to think of my children, I have to think about all of these people and the people that help us, I have to think about that. What if I do this—am I going to cause this on them? That's not where I'm at. This is not where I'm coming from. I'm not as pure as Sweet Medicine or anything like that; I don't claim to be. But what I'm saying is that if something was given that way, this guy has to do what's right. He has to tell the truth, because they were given the Arrows to stand for the truth and long life. And that's what you have to do, and if you don't have the truth and don't tell the truth, then you won't have long life. So back there, just in Custer's memoir, I mean, what he wrote is that he could hit a band on the outside and get away relatively unscathed. And these are his words. And then he said that sometimes he came between two bands and got too close to the Arrow Tipi, and then he said all ten bands came down on him. People should understand what that means today. What that means, what that meant back there, was that they could be maybe five hundred miles this way and five hundred miles this way, tipis here, how are they going to get information over there? And how did ten bands come down on him? Did he see the ten bands, or was he just boasting? I mean, but somebody had to come down on him. And the way he says it is that all they did was form a horse-shoe, and so he rode in and he rode right out. They didn't attack him or anything, they just made themselves visible on hills and all.

They should do that for the Arrows today. But that's what I keep telling them. I mean, I keep saying that—"This is what you guys have got to protect," and they would say, "Well, you're the Arrow Keeper; you'll take care of things." They just want to give it to somebody, and then they want to go do what they want to do, and they don't want to have the responsibility. They just want somebody else to take care of it. But I mean, these things were given in a sacred way, and this is why we are here today. These things were given by Maheo himself, and Sweet Medicine had to be who he was going to be. But when he gave that, there was supposed to be compassion for the people. And so if he didn't have that, then Maheo wouldn't have given him the Arrows. And then they wouldn't be here today.

Epilogue

Ne-vet-ne-ne-da-me-ohs ek-kea-so-poh-ma-oha. Don't give up. The ground rises before you. I got my dad talking, and he's upset, talking about it, and he's saying it. Ne-vet-ne-ne-da-me-ohs ek-kea-so-poh-ma-oha. I mean, that's very powerful in itself. In trying to translate it, it's not going to work. I can understand it that way. It's so difficult. By saying that Moses parted the sea, that's how difficult this thing is, okay? How do you understand Moses parted the sea, you know? It means that, like, okay, they come to that part, all right. Then the people start, I mean, by watching Moses, and the people come to that part and they see the ocean, and there's no way that we can get across. Let's go back—maybe they'll take pity on us and they won't kill all of us. You know, and so they're willing to go back. But then Moses in his belief, then whatever he does, if that's true, why then that's what happened. So that's how powerful this statement is also. You could just probably say it's as powerful as Moses parting the sea. That will be the English text words. In the Cheyenne part, the ground rises before us. Water is the only thing in the mindset of everybody that causes difficulty, and that's the only thing that will make you think. Most people associate water with problems. So "Ne-vet-ne-ne-da-me-ohs" means don't give

up. Okay, there's problems. I don't know what kind of problems, but there's problems. All right. Ne-vet-ne-ne-da-me-
ohs. Don't give up. Ek-kea-so-poh-ma-oha. The ground will
come up; the ground always rises before you.

Bill Red Hat, Albuquerque, New Mexico,

September 10, 2004

In the last chapter of his autobiography, Gerald Vizenor
reflects on the genre as a whole: "Autobiographies are imag-
inative histories; a remembrance past the barriers.... Past the
barriers his remembrance is neither sentimental nor ideological; he is a crossblood descendant of the crane and
loosens the seams in the coarse shrouds of imposed identities" (*Interior Landscapes* 262). As Vizenor suggests, the autobiographical act is an act of both memory and imagination
that seeks to liberate identity. Kathleen Mullen Sands, in
reflecting on her collaborative project with Ted Rios, also
looks beyond the barriers, saying, "Exposing the collaborative process of oral personal narrative breaks down the
binary of difference by creating a dialogic across the barriers
of alterity. In Native American collaborative biography,
teller, collector, and audience all participate" (*Telling a Good
One* 258–59). My contribution as collector in the present project most certainly has been incomplete, and yet it is my hope
that by describing Bill's and my collaborative process, I will
have given readers a sense of our cooperation in this cross-
cultural encounter. Perhaps our project will become a
resource for future Cheyenne projects.

In his narratives, Bill speaks about Cheyenne cultural survival, Cheyenne self-determination, and social justice. He
speaks a great deal about family, and about Cheyenne community and his role in this community. He speaks about
healing and his determination to help people. I hope that
readers will have gained a sense of the ways in which he
traverses the terrain between tradition and modernity. I also

hope that readers will be able to hear the quiet, patient resolve that guides him. As Vizenor says, "Language is a listener, imagination a mythic listener, a presence, being in a sound, and a word" (*Interior Landscapes* 262). Bill also speaks about Cheyenne spiritual reality. Hopefully his words will be heard by the contemporary generation of young American Indians as he affirms the continuation of Native tribal life.

The writing of this project, now complete, seems inadequate and shallow in comparison to the experience of it. For me, the experience of collaboration will always be primary. It has been several years since I last spoke with Bill Red Hat "on the record," but even though the research for this project has been completed, Bill's voice is ongoing in my life. By formalizing our conversations, I have learned the importance of listening. I have also learned that by telling stories, we articulate our place in the world. The story will not end here, because in remaining consistent with the oral tradition, it is now up to someone else to continue telling it.

Julie Cruikshank says, "social science is a form of storytelling, and the way we tell stories largely determines who will hear them" (*Life Lived Like a Story* 356). She quotes a comment by Mrs. Ned, one of the participants in her collaborative project with Yukon elders, which points to the different ways of telling stories. The context was an informal conference aimed at facilitating the exchange of ideas between archaeologists and local elders. Mrs. Ned asked: "Where do these people come from, outside? You tell different stories from us people. You people talk from paper—me, I want to talk from Grandpa" (356). Both for Mrs. Ned and for Bill, the oral tradition is educational; it is the cornerstone of the indigenous intellectual tradition.

What I hope to have accomplished in this project is the presentation of Bill's narratives as a testimony to the ongoing survival of tribal peoples. The struggle for survival means many things, including not only the survival of tribal cultures and languages, but also the struggle for self-determination so that tribal peoples can regain control of their own destinies. This pursuit takes place on many fronts, including the social, legal, political, and educational. Educating an audience is an important strategy in this regard. Educating an audience is about curtailing stereotypes and misrepresentations. It is also about affirming the fact that American Indians' tribal life continues into the present— that it is not a thing of the past.

I recall a quote I discovered on a website devoted to the works of Edward Curtis. It was in the caption to a photograph of a Sun Dance in 1900 witnessed by both George Bird Grinnell and Curtis, when Grinnell was quoted as having said, "Take a good look. We're not going to see this kind of thing much longer. It already belongs to the past." I remembered this quote when I drove to Seiling, Oklahoma, with my parents to visit the Red Hats at the ceremonial grounds shortly before the 2004 Southern Cheyenne Sun Dance was to begin. The camp lies on the outskirts of town. Our car left the paved street and bounced along a narrow dirt road lined with blackjack oaks. As we came to a clearing filled with cars, tents, tipis, and branch-covered arbors that connected in a circular pattern around a large open space, we came upon a tangible expression of the continuation of Cheyenne tribal life.

Over the course of three days we visited with the Red Hats, and I spoke with family members I had not seen in years. Bill had fulfilled his responsibilities in the Arrow Ceremony, so he had time to sit and talk. People came by frequently to visit or to bring food and gifts. Every now and then, the crier would summon individuals to the center of the camp in preparation for the completion of the Sun Dance Lodge and the beginning of the ceremony.

The evenings were a cool contrast to the heat of the day. At night we heard the crackling of fires and the banter of teenagers as they roamed along the periphery of the camp. One evening the drumming and singing began, and we watched the slow yet deliberate construction of the lodge. Another evening we congregated around the table, and as we strained to look at old family pictures aided only by the propane lantern that hung from the center of the arbor, Bill spoke of his ancestors.

On the morning we left, there were half a dozen cameras and video recorders capturing images for the remembering. Finally, Bill sang in Cheyenne, and as he sang, his voice strained, breaking near the end. That moment provoked an utter stillness as we began to say our good-byes.

In the epigraph that introduces this chapter, Bill speaks to the problem of translation. His desire to communicate propels him to use an analogy that is significant to a non-Cheyenne audience. His effort is a venture toward cross-cultural understanding. Our last recorded conversation was in Longdale on September 20, 2003. Bill, my sister, and I were sitting at the picnic table near the Arrow Tipi. Bill's grandchildren, Alicia and Ryan, were playing close by. In the following narrative, Bill addresses the imperfection of our project. I sincerely believe that in spite of the imperfections, it would be a mistake not to take such risks.

BRH: When I try to figure out something, I go down into this canyon. I go down there and I wonder if I'm doing the right thing. I have to figure out if I'm lying to myself sometimes. If I'm doing that to myself and I go down there with false things, I'm not coming back up. And it's dark and you're just sitting there praying, and you hear things moving around, and you hear someone talk in the distance, and you're wondering if you're doing the right thing; you want to know. Because then after that, after you've been down there and you believe in what you're doing, there's nothing there that can harm you. But if you don't believe in what you're doing, then you're not coming back up. [He's speaking very quietly with his eyes closed.] I have to really think. I mean, there are things you want to do and see. I would like to see my grandpa, I would like to see my dad, I would like to see my grandma. Sometimes I come out here and it's dark, and I want to see them. You ask, you cry, you beg, and you're wondering what the heck you're doing. You see them in dreams sometimes. That's good, that helps; it makes you feel a little bit better. It gives you a little hope to go on.

SMS: It sounds like it must be very hard in some ways when you're trying to help people, and it seems like it's such a struggle.

BRH: Well, it's just like what you're writing down here. I want that to be perfect, you know. And I see there's some things we shouldn't have put in there, but that's what I'm wishing for, I'm hoping for, that we do things right. But then somehow there's something that gets messed up or gets caught in the translation or whatever, or doesn't come out the same way, and so, I mean, knowing that . . .

SMS: What would make it perfect?

BRH: All the things that we said, that it got to where the reader would really understand what we're saying—that's what would make it perfect.

SMS: If all the readers were sitting with us right now, and could hear the same conversation that we hear . . .

BRH: That would be perfect. And everyone is going to have their own idea [laugh]. You want to get your story, the point, across to each person that you talk to, and you want them to hear what you're saying. But that's a lot, though. But like I say, a lot of things can go wrong, too, so that's part of this hills-and-valley thing, or bend in the road, or whatever. I wish we could all have a straight road.

You have to work things out to understand them. And it's hard, it's not easy. Just thinking about them constantly, and I'm doing that all the time. Everything. It's like when I know you girls are coming, and I know you drive safe and every-thing, but I want you guys to really get here safe, so you pray: Don't let them run into anything, don't let anything run into them. It's just something that you do, you just think about; and because of your dad and your mom, I mean, there's so much effect they have on me, too.

That's what the Cheyenne thing is like. And when you get ready to leave, the only thing you can say is "Stahot'se-wo'oms—I'll see you again." And that's what you want, that's what you really want. You don't want something to happen in between that it doesn't happen. We always say that. Stahot'sewo'oms.

Works Consulted

Basso, Keith H. *Western Apache Language and Culture: Essays in Linguistic Anthropology.* Tucson: University of Arizona Press, 1990.

Battiste, Marie, ed. *Reclaiming Indigenous Voice and Vision.* Vancouver: UBC Press, 2000.

Bennett, John W. "Applied and Action Anthropology: Ideological and Conceptual Aspects." *Current Anthropology* 37 (1996): S23–S53.

Berthrong, Donald J. *The Cheyenne and Arapaho Ordeal: Reservation and Agency Life in the Indian Territory, 1875–1907.* Norman: University of Oklahoma Press, 1976.

———. *The Southern Cheyennes.* Norman: University of Oklahoma Press, 1963.

Blaeser, Kimberly M. *Gerald Vizenor: Writing in the Oral Tradition.* Norman: University of Oklahoma Press, 1996.

Brettell, Caroline B., ed. *When They Read What We Write: The Politics of Ethnography.* Westport, Conn.: Bergin & Garvey, 1993.

Brumble, H. David, III. *American Indian Autobiography.* Berkeley: University of California Press, 1988.

———. *An Annotated Bibliography of American Indian and Eskimo Autobiographies.* Lincoln: University of Nebraska Press, 1981.

Buck, Gary. "The Southern Cheyenne, 1861–1865: The Beginning War Years." Master's thesis, Wichita State University, 1976.

Clifford, James. "Looking Several Ways: Anthropology and Native Heritage in Alaska." *Current Anthropology* 45 (2004): 5–30.

———. "On Ethnographic Allegory." In *Writing Culture: The Poetics and Politics of Ethnography,* ed. James Clifford and George E. Marcus, 98–121. Berkeley: University of California Press, 1986.

Cook-Lynn, Elizabeth. "American Indian Intellectualism and the New Indian Story." In *Natives and Academics: Researching and Writing about American Indians,* ed. Devon A. Mihesuah, 111–38. Lincoln: University of Nebraska Press, 1998.

Cruikshank, Julie. *Life Lived Like a Story: Life Stories of Three Yukon Native Elders.* Lincoln: University of Nebraska Press, 1990.

———. *The Social Life of Stories: Narrative and Knowledge in the Yukon Territory.* Lincoln: University of Nebraska Press, 1998.

Curtis, Edward S. *The Native American Indian.* Vol. 19: *The Indians of Oklahoma.* Edited by Frederick Webb Hodge. New York: Harcourt Brace Jovanovich, 1978.

Custer, George Armstrong. *My Life on the Plains; or, Personal Experiences with Indians.* 1874. Reprint, with an introduction by Edgar I. Stewart. Norman: University of Oklahoma Press, 1962.

Davis, Linda. "The Southern Cheyenne Research and Human Development Association, Inc., 1972–1980." Master's thesis, Wichita State University, 1980.

Deloria, Philip J. *Playing Indian.* New Haven, Conn.: Yale University Press, 1998.

Deloria, Vine Jr., and Clifford M. Lytle. *The Nations Within: The Past and Future of American Indian Sovereignty.* New York: Pantheon, 1984.

Dorsey, George A. *The Cheyenne: I. Ceremonial Organization.* Field Columbian Museum Publication 99. Chicago: Field Columbian Museum, 1905.

———. *The Cheyenne: II. The Sun Dance.* Field Columbian Museum Publication 103. Chicago: Field Columbian Museum, 1905.

Erdoes, Richard, and Alfonso Ortiz. *American Indian Myths and Legends.* New York: Pantheon, 1984.

Fowler, Loretta. *Tribal Sovereignty and the Historical Imagination: Cheyenne-Arapaho Politics.* Lincoln: University of Nebraska Press, 2002.

Garbarino, Merwyn S. *Native American Heritage.* Boston: Little, Brown & Co., 1976.

Geertz, Clifford. *Works and Lives: The Anthropologist as Author.* Stanford, Calif.: Stanford University Press, 1988.

Ginsburg, Faye. "The Case of Mistaken Identity: Problems in Representing Women on the Right." In *When They Read What We Write: The Politics of Ethnography,* ed. Caroline B. Brettell, 163–76. Westport, Conn.: Bergin & Garvey, 1993.

Goffman, Erving. *Frame Analysis: An Essay on the Organization of Experience.* Cambridge, Mass.: Harvard University Press, 1974.

Gould, L. Scott. "The Consent Paradigm: Tribal Sovereignty at the Millennium." *Columbia Law Review* 96 (1996): 809–902.

Grinnell, George Bird. *By Cheyenne Campfires.* New Haven, Conn.: Yale University Press, 1962.

———. *The Cheyenne Indians: Their History and Ways of Life.* 2 vols. New Haven, Conn.: Yale University Press, 1924.

———. *The Fighting Cheyennes.* Norman: University of Oklahoma Press, 1958.

———. "The Great Mysteries of the Cheyenne." *American Anthropologist,* n.s. 12, no. 4 (1910): 542–75.

Halaas, David Fridtjof, and Andrew E. Masich. *Halfbreed: The Remarkable True Story of George Bent—Caught between the Worlds of the Indian and the White Man.* Cambridge, Mass.: De Capo, 2004.

Hedburg, Donna. "Nawahwus, Bear Butte, Sacred Mountain of the Cheyenne: An Ethnohistorical and Ethnographic Account." Master's thesis, Wichita State University, 1976.

Heidegger, Martin. *Über den Humanismus.* Frankfurt: Vittorio Klostermann, 1947.

Hittman, Michael. *Corbett Mack: The Life of a Northern Paiute.* Lincoln: University of Nebraska Press, 1996.

Hoebel, E. Adamson. *The Cheyennes: Indians of the Great Plains.* New York: Holt, Rinehart and Winston, 1978.

Hoig, Stan. *The Sand Creek Massacre.* Norman: University of Oklahoma Press, 1961.

Holm, Tom. *Strong Hearts, Wounded Souls: Native American Veterans of the Vietnam War.* Austin: University of Texas Press, 1996.

Howard, Gary. "The Southern Cheyenne, 1861–1865: The Beginning War Years." Master's thesis, Wichita State University, 1976.

Hyde, George E. *Life of George Bent: Written from His Letters.* Norman: University of Oklahoma Press, 1968.

Jablow, Joseph. *The Cheyenne in Plains Indian Trade Relations, 1795–1840.* New York: J. J. Augustin, 1951.

Kappler, Charles J. *Indian Affairs: Laws and Treaties.* 2 vols. Washington, D.C.: Government Printing Office, 1904.

Kipp, Woody. *Viet Cong at Wounded Knee: The Trail of a Blackfeet Activist.* Lincoln: University of Nebraska Press, 2004.

Kollmai, Klaus. "Alcohol Abuse and the Southern Cheyenne." Master's thesis, Wichita State University, 1977.

Krupat, Arnold. *For Those Who Come After: A Study of Native American Autobiography.* Berkeley: University of California Press, 1985.

Krupat, Arnold, and Brian Swann, eds. *Here First: Autobiographical Essays by Native American Writers.* New York: Random House, 2000.

Löhn, Christina. "Prevention of Non-Insulin-Dependent Diabetes Mellitus (NIDDM) among the Southern Cheyenne: An Analysis of Its Prevalence,

Risk Factors, and Initial Treatment among Full-Blood Indians." Ph.D. dissertation, University of Kansas, 1995.

Marquis, Thomas B. *Cheyenne and Sioux: The Reminiscences of Four Indians and a White Soldier.* Edited by Ronald H. Limbaugh. Stockton, Calif.: Pacific Center for Western Historical Studies, University of the Pacific, 1973.

———. *The Cheyennes of Montana.* Algonac, Mich.: Reference Publications, 1978.

———. *Wooden Leg: A Warrior Who Fought Custer.* 1931. Reprint, Lincoln: University of Nebraska Press, 1986.

Marriott, Alice, and Carol K. Rachlin. *Dance around the Sun: The Life of Mary Little Bear Inkanish, Cheyenne.* New York: Thomas Y. Crowell, 1977.

Michelson, Truman. "The Narrative of a Southern Cheyenne Woman." *Smithsonian Miscellaneous Collections* 87 (1932): 1–13.

Mihesuah, Devon A., ed. *Natives and Academics: Researching and Writing about American Indians.* Lincoln: University of Nebraska Press, 1998.

Mihesuah, Henry. *First to Fight.* Edited by Devon A. Mihesuah. Lincoln: University of Nebraska Press, 2002.

Miller, David H. *Custer's Fall: The Indian Side of the Story.* New York: Bantam, 1957.

Momaday, N. Scott. *The Man Made of Words: Essays, Stories, Passages.* New York: St. Martin's Griffin, 1997.

———. *The Way to Rainy Mountain.* Albuquerque: University of New Mexico Press, 1969.

Monnett, John H. *Tell Them We Are Going Home: The Odyssey of the Northern Cheyennes.* Norman: University of Oklahoma Press, 2001.

Moore, John H. *The Cheyenne Nation: A Social and Demographic History.* Lincoln: University of Nebraska Press, 1987.

Nicholas, George P., and Kelly P. Bannister. "Copyrighting the Past? Emerging Intellectual Property Rights Issues in Archaeology." *Current Anthropology* 45 (2004): 327–50.

Owens, Louis. *Mixedblood Messages: Literature, Film, Family, Place.* Norman: University of Oklahoma Press, 1998.

———. *Other Destinies: Understanding the American Indian Novel.* Norman: University of Oklahoma Press, 1992.

———. *The Sharpest Sight.* Norman: University of Oklahoma Press, 1992.

Parlow, Anita, ed. *A Song from Sacred Mountain.* Pine Ridge, S.D.: Oglala Lakota Legal Rights Fund, 1983.

Powell, Peter. *Sweet Medicine: The Continuing Role of the Sacred Arrows, the Sun Dance, and the Sacred Buffalo Hat in Northern Cheyenne History.* 2 vols. Norman: University of Oklahoma Press, 1969.

Pulitano, Elvira. *Toward a Native American Critical Theory.* Lincoln: University of Nebraska Press, 2003.

Red Hat, William, Jr. Letter. *Watonga Republican,* August 11, 1994, 14.

Ridington, Robin. *Trail to Heaven: Knowledge and Narrative in a Northern Native Community.* Iowa City: University of Iowa Press, 1988.

Rios, Theodore, and Kathleen Mullen Sands. *Telling a Good One: The Process of a Native American Collaborative Biography.* Lincoln: University of Nebraska Press, 2000.

Russell, Catherine. *Experimental Ethnography: The Work of Film in the Age of Video.* Durham, N.C.: Duke University Press, 1999.

Said, Edward. *Orientalism.* New York: Vintage, 1994.

Sands, Kathleen Mullen. "Cooperation and Resistance: Native American Collaborative Personal Narrative." In *Native American Representations: First Encounters, Distorted Images, and Literary Appropriations,* ed. Gretchen M. Bataille, 134–49. Lincoln: University of Nebraska Press, 2001.

Sarris, Greg. *Keeping Slug Woman Alive: A Holistic Approach to American Indian Texts.* Berkeley: University of California Press, 1993.

Schlesier, Karl H. *Josanie's War: A Chiricahua Apache Novel.* Norman: University of Oklahoma Press, 1998.

———. "Rethinking the Midewiwin and the Plains Ceremonial Called the Sun Dance." *Plains Anthropologist* 35, no. 127 (1990): 1–27.

———. *The Wolves of Heaven: Cheyenne Shamanism, Ceremonies, and Prehistoric Origins.* Norman: University of Oklahoma Press, 1987.

———. "Zum Weltbild einer neuen Kulturanthropologie. Erkenntnis und Praxis: Die Rolle der Action Anthropology. Vier Beispiele." *Zeitschrift für Ethnologie* 105, no. 1–2 (1980): 32–66.

Schlesier, Karl H., ed. *Plains Indians, A.D. 500–1500: The Archaeological Past of Historic Groups.* Norman: University of Oklahoma Press, 1994.

Schlesier, Sibylle M. "Stahot'sewo'oms—I'll See You Again: A Study in the Working of Collaboration: The Narratives of Bill Red Hat, Cheyenne Keeper of the Arrows." Ph.D. dissertation, University of New Mexico, 2005.

Schukies, Renate. *Hüter der Heiligen Pfeile: Red Hat erzählt die Geschichte der Cheyenne.* Munich: Diederichs, 1994.

———. *Red Hat: Cheyenne Blue Sky Maker and Keeper of the Sacred Arrows.* Münster: Lit Verlag, 1993.

Seithel, Friderike. *Von der Kolonialethnologie zur Advocacy Anthropology: Zur Entwicklung einer kooperativen Forschung und Praxis von EthnologInnen und indigen Völkern.* Hamburg: Hamburg University Press, 1998.

Silko, Leslie Marmon. *Ceremony.* New York: Penguin, 1977.

Smith, Linda Tuhiwai. *Decolonizing Methodologies: Research and Indigenous Peoples*. London: Zed, 1999.

Sooktis, Rubie. *The Cheyenne Journey*. Ashland, Mont.: Religion Research Center, 1976.

Stands in Timber, John, and Margot Liberty. *Cheyenne Memories*. Lincoln: University of Nebraska Press, 1967.

Stoller, Paul. "Ethnographies as Texts / Ethnographers as Griots." *American Ethnologist* 21 (1994): 353–66.

Straus, Terry. Review of *Dance around the Sun*. *Studies in American Indian Literatures Newsletter* 2 (1978): 41–43.

Swann, Brian, and Arnold Krupat, eds. *I Tell You Now: Autobiographical Essays by Native American Writers*. Lincoln: University of Nebraska Press, 1987.

Tarn, Nathaniel. *Views from the Weaving Mountain: Selected Essays in Poetics and Anthropology*. Albuquerque: University of New Mexico, College of Arts and Sciences, 1991.

Tedlock, Dennis. *The Spoken Word and the Work of Interpretation*. Philadelphia: University of Pennsylvania Press, 983.

Trenholm, Virginia Cole. *The Arapahoes, Our People*. Norman: University of Oklahoma Press, 1970.

Tyler, Stephen A. "Post-Modern Ethnography: From Document of the Occult to Occult Document." In *Writing Culture: The Poetics and Politics of Ethnography*, ed. James Clifford and George E. Marcus, 122–40. Berkeley: University of California Press, 1986.

Vizenor, Gerald. *Dead Voices: Natural Agonies in the New World*. Norman: University of Oklahoma Press, 1992.

———. *Fugitive Poses: Native American Indian Scenes of Absence and Presence*. Lincoln: University of Nebraska Press, 1998.

———. *Interior Landscapes: Autobiographical Myths and Metaphors*. Minneapolis: University of Minnesota Press, 1990.

———. *Manifest Manners: Postindian Warriors of Survivance*. Hanover, N.H.: University Press of New England, 1994.

———. *Wordarrows: Native States of Literary Sovereignty*. Lincoln: University of Nebraska Press, 2003.

Young, Robert. *White Mythologies: Writing History and the West*. New York: Routledge, 1990.